MATILDA BETHAM-EDWARDS

NOVELIST, TRAVEL WRITER

AND

FRANCOPHILE

Second edition 2007
First published 2006

The Hastings Press
PO Box 96 Hastings TN34 1GQ
hastings.press@virgin.net
www.hastingspress.co.uk

ISBN 978-1-904109-01-3
British Library Cataloguing in Publication Data
A catalogue record for this book is available from the British Library
Printed by TJI digital, Padstow, Cornwall, England

JOAN REES is Emeritus Professor of English Literature at the University of Birmingham and a Fellow of the Royal Society of Literature. She is the author of eight books, one of which, *Shakespeare and the Story*, was awarded the Rose Mary Crawshay prize of the British Academy. Her most recent publication, *Amelia Edwards, Novelist, Traveller and Egyptologist,* is a biography of Matilda Betham-Edwards's celebrated cousin.

Cover photo: Matilda Betham-Edwards in 1911, aged 75, wearing her English and French honours. *Courtesy of Hastings Museum and Art Gallery.*

MATILDA BETHAM-EDWARDS
1836~1919

"One of the most remarkable of
the group of distinguished women
whom we now call Mid-Victorian."

SARAH GRAND

Acknowledgements

I acknowledge with gratitude permission to use materials in the keeping of Leeds University Library (Brotherton Collection Shorter Correspondence), the University of Reading, the London School of Economics and St Peter's College, Oxford. Hastings Museum, Hastings Public Library, East Sussex County Council, Suffolk County Council and Ipswich Borough Council have also been generous with help. Mrs B. M. Walthew of Orkney has kindly allowed me to quote from Sheila Kaye-Smith. Michael Bristow-Smith of St Leonards-on-Sea gave me invaluable service in introducing me to local sources of information and I owe thanks also to Mrs Judith Appleyard of St Leonards-on-Sea, Ms Elaine Hartnell, Mr C. Langdon of Young, Coles and Langdon, Hastings, Mr Michael Stone of Woodbridge, Suffolk and to Mr David Woodward of Beccles, Suffolk. To all who have taken an interest in my research and in one way or another contributed I offer my sincere thanks.

I gratefully acknowledge permission to use photographs as follows: the photographs of Matilda Betham-Edwards in age (cover and page 79) are reproduced by permission of Hastings Museum and Art Gallery; that of Matilda as a younger woman (page 27) and in later years (page 95) by permission of Hastings Library. The photograph of Amelia Edwards in maturity (page 78) is by permission of the Principal and Fellows of Somerville College, Oxford; that of her as a younger woman (page 26) by permission of the National Portrait Gallery, London.

JOAN REES

Cover: This photograph, dated 1911, shows Matilda wearing the badges of her English and French honours. The titles of the two novels of which she is most proud, *Kitty* and *The Lord of the Harvest*, are inscribed beneath it in her own hand.

FROM SUFFOLK TO FRANCE AND BACK

The story of Matilda Betham-Edwards is of a woman who was born in early Victorian England, lived through to the end of the First World War, engaged herself actively with the world of her time and for sixty years pursued two careers, one as a novelist and a second as a chronicler of French life and society. She was born a farmer's daughter in Suffolk. Her schooling finished when she was twelve but she taught herself classical and modern languages and read widely in them, she travelled in Europe and North Africa and she kept abreast of the latest intellectual movements, including those in science and theology. She tussled with questions of women's rights, the future of religion in a post-Darwinian age and issues arising from the political radicalism which she warmly and sometimes pugnaciously embraced. She did her best, in both England and France, to know everybody of interest and importance, not because she was a social climber for she never considered rank a criterion of distinction, but because she wanted to have her finger on the pulse of what was going on in the world about her and to be part of it. Her contacts and the friends she made included many of the most prominent figures of her day including George Eliot and Henry James, Kitchener, hero of the Sudan, John Morley, statesman and author, and Franz Liszt. Her autobiographical writings make up a compendium of fascinating, sometimes amusing, anecdotes and side-lights on figures well known in other contexts but caught here by one who, as she describes herself, is as "a chiel amongst ye, takin' notes". In another age she would have been a brilliant journalist and columnist. She was proud of the work she did and what she achieved and she hoped that in at least one area of her activities she would retain a hold on public memory but the hope has not been fulfilled. Posterity has forgotten her and ceased to read her books but her memory deserves to be resuscitated because she had considerable talents and character, because she was a genuine contributor to nineteenth century life and society and because hers is not only a public but also a personal story of interest in the annals of talented and ambitious Victorian women.

One of her early novels, *Kitty*, (1869), suggests that she had the potential to develop into a very good, possibly a major novelist, but in 1874/5 she made a twelve month visit to France and fell in love with it, with the result that her time and her energies were from then on split by competing claims. She did not abandon her career as a novelist but she took on the task of informing, explaining and otherwise interpreting France to her fellow-countrymen and -women, in an endeavour to dispel the ignorance and prejudice which had historically bedevilled cross-Channel relations. Her admiration of French qualities and her sympathetic understanding of French culture and customs gave her a role, she believed, as intermediary between her own country and its closest neighbour, enabling each to know the other better and thereby grow in respect and, if not love, mutual tolerance and even friendship. She never abandoned this mission or her faith in it. In 1877 she published *A Year in Western France*, the first fruits of her extended stay, and in 1917 appeared *Twentieth Century France*, her final report after forty years of travel and study. Her work was recognised as a serious contribution to Anglo-French understanding. Murray commissioned her to bring up-to-date his handbook on France and the French government made her an Officier de l'Instruction Publique de France, an honour to which she was the first English man or woman to be appointed. In the Franco-British exhibition of 1908 she showed nine volumes of the work she had produced and published over thirty-five years and was awarded a gold medal in appreciation. When she died, she was honoured by tributes on both sides of the Channel. Her attachment to France was an enrichment in all respects except the financial, but the time and energy she devoted to it was to the detriment of the other career she might have had as a distinguished novelist. From the early 1870s on, she lived a divided life, writing novels still, but pressed to write too quickly and too much by the need to earn money to support herself and to continue her French travels.

The numerous volumes of her non-fiction work, covering all aspects of French public and private life, are firmly based on first-hand knowledge and experience and lightened by her gift of easy communication, friendly without condescension, correct without pomposity. The Victorian gift for natural description is well-developed in Matilda and provides pleasurable moments in non-fiction and fiction alike. She had, moreover, a lively and vigorous mind and her French work, like everything else she wrote, is infused with the personality, interests and convictions of the writer and invigorated by a strong sense of social injustice and the evils of any social system which denies to the poor and underprivileged the expression of their full human potential. The novels, over thirty of them, weakened as they are by insufficient time and attention, have the same qualities. They are not drawing-room romances but at the centre of each there is, invariably, a challenging idea of immediate contemporary relevance which opens areas outside the round of ordinary domestic life. The foreign settings of many of them, mainly France but also Switzerland and pre-Bismarck Germany, reflect Matilda's wide travels and communicate her enjoyment and intimate knowledge of foreign lands and foreign customs — they also allow escape from the stiff and over-regulated manners of middle-class England. Right at the end of the century, in a late development of fresh creative energy, Matilda returned to home ground for inspiration and wrote six novels based on her memories of the Suffolk farmland where she was born and the farms and farming people she knew in childhood and adolescence. Like the novels with French themes or background, the Suffolk books gain from her deep commitment to the people and the land, for Suffolk never lost its hold on her loyalty and affection. Memories of early days were revived by occasional visits and Suffolk scenes and Suffolk characters were never far out of mind. They crop up from time to time even in the French books. Just as her work for Anglo-French understanding and her talents as a novelist made a dual claim on her time and efforts, so also her affections and loyalties were split between Suffolk and France, the two poles of her life.

Running throughout Matilda's career from first to last is her relationship with Amelia Blandford Edwards, cousin on her father's side, who became travel writer, novelist and, most famously, Egyptologist and founder of the Egypt Exploration Society. Amelia's father, Thomas Edwards, exceptionally among his brothers, left the family acres as a young man and chose a military career. He fought with Wellington in the Peninsular war and at the age of twenty-eight married a young Irish girl, Alicia Walpole from County Sligo. If she believed that with this marriage she was about to embark on a life of travel and adventure she was doomed to disappointment since on their way to take up a posting in India Thomas fell ill and had to leave the army and retire on half-pay. In their much reduced circumstances they set up house in a shabby area of Islington, north London, and Thomas became a bank employee. Amelia, the only child, was born fifteen years after marriage, the focus of the love and attention of both her parents, her mother in particular. She showed remarkable talents from an early age and the proud mother came to invest in her promising daughter the hopes and ambitions she had nursed for herself before Thomas's military career was cut short. Thomas, a punctilious and disciplined man, discharged his clerkly duties with conscience and regularity but he found refreshment once a year in returning with his wife and daughter to the Suffolk scenes of his youth and the brothers and sisters who lived there still. It was on one of these annual holidays that the cousins, Amelia and Matilda, first met. For Matilda, seven or eight years old at the time, it was a momentous encounter which left an impression never to be effaced.

Amelia, five years the elder, came from a quite different background from that of the small country cousin whose world had been confined to the farms and farm people in and around Ipswich. Amelia was a Londoner, brought up among the streets and the many and varied inhabitants of a big city, the daughter of a lively, drama-loving mother who early introduced her daughter to the delights of the theatre, in particular to Sadler's Wells which was near by. Her first entry into the nursery, where Matilda and the youngest of her sisters were eagerly anticipating her arrival, was itself dramatic. Boisterous and brimming with confidence, full of high spirits on her holiday outing, Amelia immediately challenged someone to dare her to throw out of the window what remained of the loaf of bread from nursery tea. She took the limelight then as she would continue to do on all the occasions in their later lives when her path and Matilda's crossed. From that first meeting was born a relationship which was marked on Matilda's side by admiration of the vibrant and attractive personality of her cousin, compounded with jealousy of the attention and admiration she invariably attracted. From then on her sense of herself became inextricably bound up with her sense of Amelia. Amelia for her part was always, with very few exceptions, uncommunicative about her personal feelings but, some minor tensions apart, she appears to have felt affection for Matilda and to have been in some degree protective towards her, encouraging her writing and on one occasion at least offering her advice. Matilda's adoption of a family name, Betham, to add to their common patronymic irritated Amelia by risking (and causing) unnecessary confusion of their identities but the cousins retained contact with each other up to the time of Amelia's death in 1892, some twenty years before Matilda herself died. Meetings were infrequent in the busy later years but Amelia spent three weeks with Matilda, just before in 1890 she went off on a lecturing tour of the United States on behalf of the Egypt Exploration Society. The tour was a triumphant success but the strain of it hastened her death at the age of sixty-one.

The two women followed in some respects parallel careers. Both were novelists and both developed a deep attachment to another country: Matilda to France, Amelia to Egypt. Subsequently they devoted their talents and their time to the task of widening knowledge and understanding of the people and society of their chosen lands but they apportioned their energies differently. Until she went to Egypt for the first and only time, in 1873, Amelia concentrated on her career as travel writer and novelist. Her eight novels are rich with evidence of a highly intelligent and widely cultivated mind and her major travel books are still widely read and admired: *Untrodden Peaks and Unfrequented Valleys* is a well-informed and attractive account of what was then virtually a pioneering expedition in the Dolomites, undertaken with a friend, while *A Thousand Miles up the Nile*, the story of her Egyptian journey, is a book of great distinction, a work of both charm and scholarship. After Egypt, Amelia wrote one more novel but from then on she gave her time and her talents exclusively to promoting the work of the Egypt Exploration Society. Matilda, on the other hand, continued to write her novels side by side with her work on behalf of France and Anglo-French relations and inevitably they suffered from the division of effort. Her own intelligence and cultivation are not in doubt but the need to earn money to support her French work draws heavily on the intellectual and physical resources which might have gone into the writing of her novels. The evidence in some books of her real talent as a novelist is striking enough to make her choice of a double career a matter of some regret.

Matilda herself did not regret it. In happier moods she dwelt on the many and rewarding friendships she had made and of which she could count an impressive tally but a sense that she had missed the due acknowledgement of her talents and achievements in both her fields, as Francophile and novelist, was the cause of recurrent bouts of bitterness in later life which developed into an obsessive fear that her name and her life's work would be forgotten. The fear came to focus on jealousy of Amelia, her success and the fame her efforts had won her, and in 1900, eight years after Amelia's death, long suppressed feelings engendered back in childhood days came to the surface in an astonishingly venomous attack in one of the Suffolk novels. It is a striking exposure of the negative elements in Matilda's relation with her brilliant cousin. Recognition of Amelia's qualities and gratitude for the stimulus of her example had always been mingled with envy and irritation at the admiration she evoked in others. At one point the pressure of competing feelings becomes uncontainable and in *A Suffolk Courtship* she gives it full vent.

The intertwining stories of these two women, in some respects closely connected and yet in others very different in temperament and talents, adds another layer to the record of nineteenth-century women of brains and initiative who somehow fought their way through obstruction and obfuscation to find means of expressing their talents and their energies. They triumphed, though for both there was a cost, and they both laid claim to be remembered for what they had accomplished. "My work will, I hope, in a sense go on forever", Amelia told an American friend, referring not to personal accomplishments but to the impetus she had given to Egyptology in this country and her hope that it would continue and gather force. As for her writing, she knew that *A Thousand Miles up the Nile* was in a class of its own. "This is the most important of my books", she wrote, "and the one by which I most hope to be remembered". Matilda's hopes for the future, equally sincere, were less confident. Her long labour of preparation for an *entente cordiale* which she prefigured long before 1904 involved her with the living society of troubled, turbulent, ever-changing France not the dead world of Amelia's Ancient Egypt. She knew that she could expect nothing other than that, sooner or later — and probably quite soon — what she had to say would become outdated. She hoped for some credit nonetheless and she hoped also that at least one of her novels would survive. She was right to identify *Kitty* as the best of them but the story of her life and work goes well beyond any one item and in the centenary of her Golden Jubilee — one hundred and fifty years since the publication of her first novel, *The White House by the Sea* — a retrospect and an assessment are no more than her due.

Chapter One

BEGINNINGS

Matilda Edwards, or Betham-Edwards as she later called herself, was born at Westerfield Hall, Suffolk on March 4th, 1836, the fifth child and fourth daughter of Edward Edwards and his wife, Barbara Betham. The 1851 Census lists six children, five girls of whom Matilda was the second youngest, and an older boy. In reminiscences of childhood Matilda refers once to a younger brother but he was presumably dead by 1851, his death perhaps one of the "sadnesses" which she said punctuated her childhood. Among these was the death of her mother when she was twelve.

In 1851 Edward Edwards was farming 186 acres and employed six men. He came of a farming family but his wife's connections were more literary. Her grandfather, vicar of Stonham Aspal, Suffolk, later of Stoke Lacy near Hereford, was the compiler of *Genealogical Tables of the Sovereigns of the World* and her uncle, Sir William Betham, Ulster King of Arms, was the author of historical and antiquarian studies of the Celts. The most interesting member of this family, however, the one with most influence on Matilda and after whom she was named, was her aunt and godmother, Mary Matilda Betham (1776-1852). Mary Matilda was a poet and a miniature painter with some reputation in both arts. She moved in a distinguished literary circle which included Southey and Coleridge and both the Lambs. Charles Lamb, reflecting on the large family from which she came — she was one of fifteen children — called them "the measureless Bethams" and claimed that he knew "a quarter of a mile of them"! Coleridge addressed a poem to her in which he exhorted her to "Be wise! Be bold! Fulfil my auspices!" but hastily tempered this by adding that as a "meek woman" she must be "wisely bold".

Whether or not Mary Matilda was meek she was certainly talented and exercised her gifts. In 1804 she published *A Biographical Dictionary of Celebrated Women of Every Age and Country*, among whom she included Mary Wollstonecraft, then only recently dead. When in 1880 her niece and namesake, Matilda, by that time a well-known and prolific writer on her own account, published *Six Life Stories of Famous Women* she very properly included Mary Matilda in the list. She must indeed have derived a great deal from this godmother, a close-to-home example of a woman who had won a place of honour in a discriminating circle and whose correspondence stimulated her with talk of books and gossip about the literary figures she knew. She seems to have been a delightful person. Amelia Edwards, whose aunt she also was, preserves a charming reminiscence of how:

> She generally carried a big basket and a Brobdignag umbrella. From the depths of this umbrella she would sometimes bring out some magazine of many years gone by, and read aloud, with not ungraceful emphasis, a poem of her own ... Her eccentricities of dress were proverbial. My father [Matilda's uncle] once met her in a frequented London thoroughfare serenely walking in crimson velvet slippers, and followed by a train of little ragamuffins, to whose "chaff" she was good-humouredly indifferent.

The anecdote vividly recalls Mary Matilda and also gives a glimpse of family life in the Islington home when Amelia was young, a home which became very familiar to cousin Matilda when in late adolescence she came to London for the first time and spent evenings with aunt and uncle and Amelia. On Mary Matilda's death Matilda annexed the Betham name to add to her own plain Edwards and presented herself to the world as Matilda Betham-Edwards. She was proud of the Huguenot descent of her mother's family and once had a family tree drawn up which traced the lineage back to Ralph de Betham in the reign of Henry II. It pleased her greatly to associate herself with her Betham forebears but the hyphenated name was to cause her embarrassment, even distress. Nevertheless she would not relinquish it.

Lamb evidently respected Mary Matilda not least, perhaps, for her eccentricities. He offered to help with proof correction of her poem "The Lay of Marie", though he never quite got round to it as he never quite got round to sharing a legacy with her. A small amount had been left to Charles and Mary Lamb by one of the Betham sisters. As Amelia tells this story:

> Touched even to tears, he begins by disclaiming the legacy. At first he will have none of it — "not a penny". Next he proposes to "halve it" with [Mary] Matilda, who was the least prosperous of her family. Lastly, as the ink cools in his pen, he proposes that his sister and he shall share it with Matilda in three equal parts. The letter occupies the first page of a sheet of foolscap. Had he written a few more lines and turned the leaf, he would probably have ended by taking the whole.

Westerfield Hall, Matilda Betham-Edwards's Suffolk birthplace
Photo: Margaret Simpson

More seriously, Amelia adds: "The letter is curiously illustrative of the warmth, impulsiveness, and irresolution of the writer". Certainly it gives another insight into the warm — and in these instances impecunious — côterie in which the younger Matilda and her cousin first nurtured the seeds of their own talents.

Amelia was born and brought up amid the swirl of London life; Matilda on a farm in rural Suffolk with all the limitations of background and company which that entailed. The death of her mother would inevitably have been a severe loss, though the relationship seems never to have been close, unlike that between Alicia Edwards and the precociously gifted Amelia whom she adored and whose developing talents she fostered and encouraged. The mother-daughter relationship was a strong influence on Amelia but Matilda offers no reminiscence of her own mother except that she was "a beautiful, refined, and for her day, highly educated woman". As for brothers and sisters, there is singularly little reference to them in the copious autobiographical anecdotes and reminiscences which figure largely in Matilda's work. The youngest sister (not mentioned by Matilda) became a particular favourite of cousin Amelia who referred to her as the "very young and very dear Alfreda" and there were deaths and marriages. Matilda refers to an unnamed brother-in-law and two young nephews. Beyond that and a brief period when Matilda lived with an unmarried sister, their lives are a blank. It may be that some chronic physical weakness dogged them and Matilda herself had periods of sometimes severe ill-health. Alone among her family, however, she had the fortitude to survive into the twentieth century and she lived to be eighty-two.

At the age of ten she was sent to a day-school where she was taught by a woman who was a devotee of grammar and of French grammar in particular. This was nothing but good fortune for Matilda as the teacher was well qualified and her enthusiasm planted the germ of the equally passionate interest which her pupil came in adult life to take in France and French affairs. In one of Matilda's early novels, *Dr Jacob* of 1864, set largely in Frankfurt, there appears a real-life character, Fraulein Fink, who, like Matilda's French teacher, runs a school for girls. Like her predecessor in Suffolk, she has a passion for language, German this time, and in recreating her within the novel Matilda evidently drew on memories of her own early schooling as well as upon the more immediate model. Affectionate memory, tinged with some gentle mockery, colours the portrait. After the mother's death Matilda seems to have left school and her education was left very much to what she cared to pick up for herself. The widowed Edward Edwards was, so she tells us, a loving father but not himself intellectual. Nevertheless the house's small collection of books included copies of the Bible and Shakespeare and Milton as well as of Walter Scott and other classics, among them *The Spectator* and *The Idler* and Smollett's translation of *Don Quixote*. Matilda read them greedily, over and over again. This was an education in itself but, beyond this, her freedom to follow her own devices allowed her to acquire a precocious knowledge of life and human behaviour as she studied the lives and characters of the farmers and farmhands amongst whom she lived. Her later career as a writer was to be built on these foundations: a love of literature and what she describes as her "stock-in-trade", knowledge culled from experience of all sorts and conditions of life and a range of acquaintance from the lowest to the highest. How carefully and appreciatively she studied her Suffolk surroundings and the farmers and farm workers who lived there becomes fully apparent in the six novels based on Suffolk rural life which she wrote between 1899 and 1906, but an attractive evocation of the Suffolk life she knew in her early years appears in an article of 1893 written for *The New England Magazine*. The article is intended primarily as a memoir of Amelia, who had died in the previous year, and it is one of several pieces written at various dates in which Matilda draws on her memories of her cousin, and especially of the childhood and early adult years when they saw a great deal of each other and shared experiences in common. She made a special visit to the home ground in preparation for the article and in nostalgic mood sought out the houses and well-known spots which had once been all the world she knew. She delights to see again the Swan Inn in Needham Market and to wander through its numerous passages and the old rooms redolent of memories of long past lives. She remembers the wild flowers which used to grow round about, naming with love the unostentatious riches of meadow and lane: cowslips and marigolds, wild roses, wood anemones and ladysmock, ragged robin, honeysuckle and wild rose. With fresh pleasure she renews acquaintance with Creeting St Peter — "rusticity itself" — once home of Uncle William and Aunt Maria, and exclaims at the beauty of Coddenham — "as pretty a village as England can show ... indeed a gem of gems". She recreates in imagination the typical farmhouse interior she used to know:

> The kitchen, spacious, spick and span, from the roof hanging home-cured hams pickled in old harvest beer and spice, the frothing milk-pails being brought in from the dairy, the "keeping-room" with its appetizing board, everything of the best and everything home-made.

Such scenes figure again and again in the novels but they gain a particular piquancy here from the explicitly personal tone. In her much-travelled adulthood Matilda never weakened in her love for her native county and the *New England* article is an affecting tribute to its lasting hold on her.

Much as she loved Suffolk, however, thoughts of a future living to make sharpened the need for further education and Matilda was enrolled as a pupil-teacher in a seminary for young ladies: Mimosa House in Peckham, London. In her volume *Reminiscences* (1898) she can hardly find words harsh enough to describe "the unutterably low ethic standards and intellectual dead level" of life behind "those ever-abhorred doors". As a pupil-teacher she paid a small sum for board and lodging and taught the junior pupils for two or three hours every morning. In return she received lessons from "approved masters" in music, drawing and dancing. She wrote:

> It may be asked what in Heaven's name a studious and rather severe young person [herself] should want of a dancing master? The fact is, two maternal aunts, great authorities on such matters, had laid it down as an axiom that "dancing implies birth and breeding".

The aunts, two of Lamb's "quarter of a mile" of Bethams, may or may not have included Mary Matilda, but in any case young Matilda soon detached herself from an arrangement she had only entered into to please them and she learned to play the piano instead. The drawing lessons offered were a waste of time but the music teacher had some qualification and was a conscientious teacher, good enough at any rate to encourage in Matilda a deep and abiding love of music. This did not mitigate her overall verdict that the school was characterised by an "utter want of education, either religious, moral or intellectual". In its absence, all kinds of evils flourished. Snobbishness and bullying were perhaps to be expected but Matilda's account of the behaviour of the older girls gives a picture of Victorian young womanhood which is a far cry from the conventional image: "Vices with which they ought to have been absolutely unfamiliar, were openly discussed, and in language that savoured of the gutter...Where had girls of well-to-do middle-class parents learned such abominations?" Even worse than the "ingrained depravity" was a callous bullying which was not only unchecked but was actively encouraged by the Principal and head governess. This was not Dotheboys Hall but it was a house "of evil memory", nevertheless; and Matilda rejoices, "that we might nowadays search the United Kingdom through without finding its counterpart."

Distasteful as life in Mimosa House was, the Peckham months were not entirely barren for during that time Amelia and Matilda were able to renew and develop the acquaintance which had begun when they were children and Matilda had looked on as the lively and irrepressible cousin, on annual visits with her parents, stirred up the households of Suffolk aunts and uncles with her high spirits, love of fun and daring. At the time when Matilda was in Peckham Amelia was toying with the idea of a musical career, studying hard, taking and giving lessons and playing the organ for a local church. It was not a happy period for her. She was many-gifted, a talented artist as well as an accomplished musician, and she had already had juvenile work published; but the abundance of promise created a problem of choice. Since her parents were not in a position to provide for her future she had to find means of supporting herself, and where the best prospects lay was doubtful. Marriage was, of course, the obvious alternative to a career and it was probably at the instigation of anxious parents that at the age of about twenty she entered into an engagement; but her heart was not in it and she soon broke it off. She seems to have harboured a liking for an Irish cousin but the unfortunate engagement prevented anything developing from this. In her early twenties she became deeply attached to a Frenchman, Emile Stéger — "the dearest and most intimate of friends", she called him — but he also drops out of sight and the question of possible marriage does not arise again. Writing soon after Amelia's death, Matilda makes oblique reference to Mr Bacon, the jilted fiancé, and perhaps to other failed suitors too. Amelia had, she writes, "the perilous dower of personal fascination ... and it was hardly her fault if she at times awakened interest or affection she could not return". This cryptic remark remains undeveloped but the quality of "personal fascination" — or, in today's word, charisma — evidently made a great impression on Matilda. She was to identify it again in Liszt when she encountered him years later and then, as in her comment on Amelia, she seems to regard it as a burden rather than a source of pleasure or pride: it threatened too much involvement in other lives, too many claims for attention, and it infringed personal freedom. Amelia refused to become bound and entered into no commitments. Watchful young Matilda looked on and took note as her cousin faced her dilemmas and made her choices.

There were affinities between the cousins but also striking differences, not least in appearance. Matilda describes Amelia as she first saw her as a tall girl "with regular features, pale, clear complexion and abundance of dark hair hanging in pigtails down her back". An early and rare full-face photograph shows a strikingly confident young woman poised with pen in hand and ready to challenge the world with force of personality and intelligence. Her more usual pose in three-quarter profile, chosen perhaps as the most flattering angle, shows her in her maturity as a handsome woman with fine eyes and mouth, as U.S. journalists observed during her American tour of 1890-91, but then as earlier it was evidently personality, or what Matilda called "personal fascination", rather than harmony of features in itself which accounted for the effect she made at twenty as at sixty. Matilda's appearance was always less striking. In a photograph taken when she was about twenty she appears as a plain young woman, but her eyes are alert and penetrating and she has a notably strong chin. What she calls "a slight obliquity of vision" affected her in early years but this was later corrected and in pictures of middle and late life she looks out from under heavy lids with bright, keen eyes. A journalist who visited her in 1891 describes her as of medium height, slender figure, fair complexion, hazel eyes, a small head and a mass of thick dark hair. Scrupulously neat, in her photographs she holds herself firmly, a woman keyed up for action with a mind and a will of her own, whose pose in her latest years confidently asserts the honour she feels is due to her life's work. Her appearance improved with age, but in the early days her less dynamic looks, combined with the five years' difference in growth and development between her and Amelia, emphasised the difference in their status. In response she sharpened her observation and her judgement of the events and the people surrounding her.

The Edwards's house in London was, first, 1 Westmoreland Place, City Road, and, later, what Matilda describes as "a much pleasanter house" in Wharton Street, Percy Circus. Matilda came to know both houses well and during her visits there she absorbed the unfamiliar urban surroundings with enthusiasm. She never lost what much later she described as:

> An ineradicable affection for the proximity of Colebrook Row with its associations of Charles Lamb, of Sadler's Wells dear to Shakespearians, of the sombre Irvingite church, and even the dusty little gardens of Percy Circus and Myddleton Square.

It was pleasant on summer evenings to stroll past Charles Lamb's house by the New River, to admire the High Street (which in her novel, *Bridget*, she describes as "that Vanity Fair of unaristocratic London") and enjoy "the stir and metropolitan aspect of Angel corner!" Indoors, round the Islington fireside on evenings when she was free of duty at the detested Peckham seminary, she shared the company of the ex-soldier uncle, his lively Irish wife and the brilliant daughter, who was for both parents the compensation for their thwarted expectations, and she could watch with keen interest as Amelia struggled to find a way to her own kind of fulfilment, drawn as she was on the one hand by social pressure towards marriage and on the other by her need to give full expression to her gifts in an independent career. Disappointed in her hopes of finding an opening in music or in art, Amelia finally made up her mind that her future lay in writing and her first novel, *My Brother's Wife*, was published in 1855. She joined the staff of the *Saturday Review* and the *Morning Post* and became a busy and successful journalist, at the same time accepting publishers' commissions as they came along and producing more fiction. Her fourth novel, *Barbara's History* (1864), established her reputation as a novelist, to which a few years later her travel books and her gifts as a short-story writer added fresh lustre. Egyptology and the devotion of her literary and other talents to its service came later.

Meanwhile Matilda launched herself. Inspired, as it may well be, by Amelia's example and thinking it never too soon to begin to catch up, she had begun work on her first novel while she was still at home in Suffolk and, in 1857, when she was barely twenty-one, *The White House by the Sea* was published. It concerns a sixteen-year old girl (about Matilda's age when she began it) living an isolated and reclusive life with her widowed father who suffers from an incapacitating illness (again reflecting her own experience). Like Matilda (and Amelia) she has a passion for knowledge and without companions or instructors she teaches herself Latin and Greek and educates herself as widely as she can in whatever time she has available. Neither Amelia nor Matilda owed much to formal education, though Amelia's mother did at times engage tutors for her daughter. On the whole Amelia preferred to teach herself as Matilda perforce, having little alternative, also did. The novel's heroine so far mirrors the experience of the two Edwards cousins, but more dramatic adventures are to follow. Her uneventful life comes to an end when during a storm she goes out alone at night to help a party of smart pleasure seekers whose boat has got into difficulties. They take refuge in her cottage and she becomes involved in love-affairs, her own and other people's, which lead among other things to an elopement and a dramatic night-time scene of an attempted suicide. The young author having rounded off these exciting events with appropriate pairings, she has to call on the good offices of the family grocer to get the manuscript to London for there was no parcel post in those days. The manuscript itself had received special attention, as she confided to an American interviewer many years later: "I had, you may be amused to hear", she said, "taken the precaution to have the paper smoked — my brother obliging with his pipe". This was so that the publisher should think the unknown author was a man. "I found afterwards", she went on, "that even if they had done so it would have been anything but an advantage. Just at that time all the publishers were particularly inclined to pay attention to a young lady, especially from the country. They were all hoping that another Charlotte Brontë might turn up". Smith, Elder perhaps shared the hope; certainly they accepted the novel straight away and can never have regretted it since it remained in print during most of Matilda's life.

The White House by the Sea contains a generous — over-generous — helping of romantic motifs as Matilda later confessed, excusing youthful indulgence as a reaction to the wretchedness of life at the Peckham seminary; but in spite of this (or perhaps because of it) the novel turned out to have an astonishingly long life. It was frequently reprinted and when Tauchnitz reissued it in time to mark fifty-five years after first publication, Matilda was overjoyed and could not resist a gloating comparison with other novelists, more lauded in their time, whose works had come and gone: "How many dazzling reputations have vanished meanwhile!" she crows to her friend and literary confidant Frederic Harrison. Fear of being overshadowed and overlooked was an obsession of later years and she basked uninhibitedly in the notice her first novel brought her. By then she was prepared to forget her earlier reservations and to claim it as characteristic in embryo of the work of her maturity: "The child was mother to the woman", she told Harrison in a letter of 1913. "I find in glancing through these simple pages that at 21 I was very much what I am half a century later". In fact, in spite of its obvious demerits, *The White House by the Sea* is a remarkably assured and even sophisticated production for so young an author. Apart from the standard classics she read in her father's house, Matilda had evidently imbibed and learnt from contemporary fiction, courtesy of the obliging librarian at Ipswich to whom she was indebted for a generous allowance of books. She claims in her age that *The White House* still represents her constant ideas and opinions and it is indeed true that themes which are to emerge strongly throughout her life are sounded already in this first book, notably anti-clericalism and contempt for hypocritical, middle-class morality.

Matilda had made her very first visit to London in 1851 and on that occasion had taken another early step towards a literary career. She saw the young Queen open Parliament and heard one of Dickens's famous readings, on this evening the story of Little Em'ly. "A commanding but rather dandyish figure", as she describes him, he was dressed in black velvet and much befrilled and be-diamonded in his usual style for these occasions. At fifteen Matilda showed already what was to be a characteristic alacrity in seizing opportunities. The thrill of seeing and hearing the great man in person inspired her to submit to him a poem entitled *The Golden Bee*, a vigorously-told, dramatic story of shipwreck, heroism and an unexpected happy ending. He accepted it for *All the Year Round* and sent her a fee of five pounds, together with an encouraging letter. This was a much-prized accolade and she quoted Dickens's approval of her early effort when many years later she solicited a publisher's interest in a collection of her poems. *The Golden Bee* was popular and she continued to reprint this early effort in the several collections of her verse which appeared later.

By 1858 both Amelia and Matilda were well-launched on a life of authorship. Their kinship was a bond which sometimes chafed. The common surname and especially the B of both their middle names — Blandford (which Amelia commonly used in her publications) and Betham — led to endless confusion when readers and reviewers ascribed the work of one to the other, a muddle which angered Amelia, who felt she had first claim to the B, and was a cause of lasting mortification to Matilda when she was congratulated on work which was in fact her cousin's. In her autobiographical compilations Matilda names herself and Amelia as "the two Dromios", referring to the servants in *The Two Gentlemen of Verona* whose common name causes all sorts of comic mistakes and misadventures; but the coincidence of the B's was, in reality, a far from comic matter to either of the cousins and they were keen to separate their identities. "We never consulted each other about literary work or business", Matilda insists, "Each went her own way unfettered by loving interference, counsel or criticism". "A certain measure of reserve", as she puts it, "and absolute freedom of action" characterised their relationship. Their paths in adult life crossed only occasionally as each pursued her individual life, moving in different circles, cultivating different interests and producing very different books; but close acquaintance with Amelia at the time when she was writing her early novels seems to leave one or two traces in Matilda's own early work. The attractive but deeply flawed cleric who is at the centre of Matilda's novel, *Dr Jacob* derives directly from an encounter she had in Germany, but she may have been encouraged to develop her portrait of him by Amelia's picture of an equally brilliant and fascinating but corrupt clergyman, Xavier Hamel, in her book *Hand and Glove* (1858). A curious late echo of *Hand and Glove* occurs in Matilda's *Anglo-French Reminiscences* of 1900, where Matilda relates an anecdote about "the great mathematician, Sylvester ... the greatest expert in modern algebra", whom she once met and of whom she records that he "greatly prided himself upon his vocal accomplishments", especially his "upper C". Accommodating hostesses would, she says, go so far as to provide piano accompaniment while again and again the professor repeated his favourite "high C". A very similar story receives richly comic embellishment in the musical ambitions of Amelia's M. Delahaye, a character in *Hand and Glove*, who, oblivious of the fact that his elderly voice has retained no vestige of tunefulness and is "ear-rending to the last degree", practises each day at dawn and prides himself especially on his "low B". That Amelia and Matilda both at different times in their lives met eccentric characters with the same vocal vanity is possible, but it seems more likely that Matilda's anecdote derives from a confused recollection of an early reading of Amelia's book, or perhaps of a fireside chat in youthful Islington days when the cousins talked together of what they were doing and what they planned to do. Matilda's memory was unreliable in later life and if she appropriated her cousin's story it was at least a spur to creative embellishment of her own.

From the time of Amelia's first visit to Paris with her father when she was a girl, until the 1873 visit to Egypt satisfied her wanderlust once and for all, Amelia was an enthusiastic and adventurous traveller. She went to Paris in 1853 and 1854 and it was there she met Emile Stéger. She met him again in Paris in 1855 and in company with a few other friends they talked, smoked and drank champagne in what she described as a "thoroughly happy" summer. Although after that M. Stéger and the briefly joyous relationship drop out of sight, Amelia continued to explore France and to go on afterwards to Germany and Switzerland. The high spirits which had enlivened — and alarmed — the children at nursery tea in Westerfield and the bachelor uncles and maiden aunts in their Suffolk villages were evidently by no means exhausted in these years. She took up pistol-shooting and riding, became knowledgeable about wines and vintages and, alert to everything that came her way, she soaked up the material which she would afterwards use in her novels.

Matilda followed her example and in her twenties became familiar with Germany, Austria and France. By what means or by whom her travels were financed does not appear. Possibly she had been left a legacy by her mother or perhaps by Mary Matilda, who died in 1852, or she may have taken work as a pupil-teacher, a life which she writes about, with a sharp appreciation of its hardships, in the novel *Brother Gabriel* (1878). Matilda was never a wealthy woman but provided she had enough to live on she seems to have been unconcerned about money. She had sufficient, at least, to maintain herself and sooner or later introduced herself to respectable middle-class or slightly higher circles. "Abroad" seems to have held no fears or problems at any stage for either Amelia or Matilda and Matilda took to foreign travel avidly, delighting in different environments and customs. Though there was no M. Stéger in her life and her adventures were less unconventional than those of her still exuberant cousin, she found drama enough in the encounters she had and plenty of material to enlarge her ideas and her experience.

Her first stay was in Würtemberg at a time when "a dozen charming little kingdoms" still had their own character before unification "lopp[ed] off every vestige of spontaneousness and originality". Matilda never ceased to regret the disappearance of the Grand Duchies with their miniature courts, their artistic life and their local customs and one such state is the main setting of *Felicia*, a novel of 1875. Matilda presents it as a community devoted to music where citizens of all classes flock to listen to the latest as well as the most familiar music and judiciously appraise it. Amelia wrote of a similar small state in *Barbara's History* (1864), though her appreciation, unlike Matilda's, is tinged with some amusement at the pretensions of the miniature court. The Franco-Prussian war of 1870 and its consequences radically changed attitudes to Germany and Matilda particularly resented the annexation of Alsace-Lorraine, where she had friends but, back in the late 50s and early 60s, she found southern Germany delightful. She went on to Frankfurt and enjoyed the glitter and the spectacle of its wealth as well as the memories of Goethe's youth which it held. She paid a second visit in 1862. In the same year she published a novel, *John and I*, her first major book since *The White House by the Sea* and the first of what were to be many novels with a foreign setting. *John and I* has for background the Germany she was beginning to know well.

It concerns an Englishman — handsome, talented and attractive to women —but, it turns out, rather lacking in moral fibre. He marries the widowed Baroness Marie, a German aristocrat some years older than himself. Marie's young daughter, Hermine, falls in love with him and, after resisting the feeling for some time, he has to confess that he feels attracted towards her. He repents of his weakness and his faithfulness to Marie never comes into serious question. He continues to adore her but she, learning of the momentary wavering, cannot brook even the slightest deviation from the most absolute and high-minded devotion to her and she ruthlessly casts him off. Eventually, after much misery all round, they are reconciled. The moralising is tiresome and the characters unconvincing but the novel is worth noticing because of what lies at the bottom of it. Clumsy as the treatment may be, Matilda is implicitly challenging conventional morality by applying to a man the hypersensitive sexual code traditionally applied to women. John is not unfaithful in fact but briefly wavers in mind and for his weakness is ostracised as severely as any allegedly "impure" woman might be. It is an advanced position and gives notice that from the beginning Matilda as novelist will be prepared to open her fiction to challenging ideas.

Though Matilda is bold in the implicit criticism of common assumptions which she makes, the novel itself, unfortunately, is not bold enough to be effective, and the presence of John's brother Hendy, a moralising prig, smothers whatever vitality it might have had. Some of the points are sharp enough, however, especially those concerned with Hermine, the young woman who loves John. Hermine is a proto-feminist complaining that:

> Girls are not allowed to have souls! – a pattern is put
> before them of words, thoughts, and actions, which,
> if they transgress, they are branded at once; and being
> a girl I am not at liberty to think for myself but must
> accept such a life as the world thinks fit and proper.

She complains of having nothing to occupy her:

> Oh! Who can wonder that so many girls are wrapped
> up in petty vanities or selfish worldliness? Who can
> wonder that so many are coquettes or fools? What
> are women born with minds for if they are perverted
> to such uses?

This is a chord which Matilda's novels strike many times. Hermine tries to think and act for herself and when John is taken ill she endangers her reputation to nurse him; but sexual injustice asserts itself in the end when the Baroness forgives John his lapse but Hermine is not allowed to find happiness or ever again regain esteem or dignity. Similar advances and retreats mark Matilda's presentation of her women characters throughout her life as aspiration to freedom of thought and activity conflicts with traditional ideals of femininity. Though she shares the one, she cannot quite shake off the other.

In Frankfurt Matilda boarded in the home of an English clergyman, a Jew who had converted to Christianity and who had been sent to Frankfurt by a society dedicated to the conversion of the Jews. Whether he had any success in his mission or not Matilda never learned, but from him she heard the story of another clergyman who had come to Frankfurt to raise money for a self-imposed undertaking even less promising than that of her host: he was to conduct a crusade against Judaism in Jerusalem itself. Christian Frankfurt, Matilda heard, had welcomed this man with open arms. He was not young but he was handsome, a brilliant orator and in every way fascinating: "Women, one and all, from the titled dame to the washerwoman, lost their heads about this irresistible sexagenarian". Matilda too was fascinated and the story inspired her to write another Germany-based novel, *Dr Jacob*, published in 1864. Its theme is in some respects similar to that of the earlier one. John's story is wrapped up in a great deal of mawkishness but essentially it is one of a man whose talents and virtues are defeated by flaws of character. The potential of Dr Jacob is far greater than John's, his flaws more serious and his fall greater and more conclusive. This theme of potential excellence vitiated by moral weakness is one that was exercising Amelia also, most notably in the story of Xavier Hamel, the devastatingly attractive ex-convict of *Hand and Glove* (1858), and that of William Trefalden, the clever and ambitious solicitor who takes to fraud in *Half a Million of Money* (1865). Possibly it was a topic the cousins had discussed together but, if so, they chose to emphasise different elements in it. Amelia's characters are men who, cramped in their sphere of action by restrictive social conditions, take to criminality in order to claim for themselves what they think their talents deserve. In their defiance of conventional restriction they attain, moral considerations apart, something like heroic stature. Matilda also is fierce against social injustice especially in relation to women, but at this stage of her career her stories remain on a personal level with little political resonance. A few years later that situation will change and under the stimulus of her love for France her novels will generate a considerable political charge.

For the time being the emphasis is on Dr Jacob as an individual. Matilda depicts him as a man idolised by society who delights to repay hospitality with princely prodigality, bestowing jewels and other costly presents on men, women and babies alike. Inevitably the bubble bursts and Dr Jacob is forced to flee Frankfurt, head over heels in debt, having squandered in fine living and ostentatious generosity the money which has been collected for the conversion of the Jews. He is a sybarite, a lover of the good life at other people's expense, a gambler, a womaniser who may or may not have committed adultery and who is on the verge of seducing an implausibly angelic eighteen year-old. The novel tantalises throughout with dark suggestions of a murky past and hints of dastardly deeds to come but, in fact, nothing quite disastrous is allowed to happen. Dr Jacob escapes from Frankfurt and lives a soberer life thereafter. His maverick vitality is not entirely crushed, however. Reviewing his life in his enforced retirement, he reassesses his religious outlook in the light of new ideas which are beginning to circulate, according to which the Christian story is to be rejected in favour of a view in which "each soul is no property of man, but a particle of the great cycle of Being". He finds these ideas "grand and enthralling" but dismisses them as ultimately unsatisfying and he returns to "the cross and the Man of God". This passage is characteristic in that it ventures beyond accepted parameters and introduces ideas on the edge of contemporary thinking. Characters in later novels will follow Dr Jacob's train of thought or be attracted to other versions of it, as Matilda prompts her readers to take note of new ideas and reject quiescent acceptance of old ones.

The novel opens the door for questioning of religious orthodoxy, but one firmly-rooted conventional doctrine appears on the surface to remain here undisturbed — that of female passivity and subordination. A Dr Paulus who figures in the novel is contemptuous of a fellow clergyman because he consults his wife and respects her opinions. His own wife is a chronic invalid who never leaves her room and spends most of her time in bed, utterly incapacitated for any exertion, mental or physical. Dr Paulus dotes on her and waits on her and the children are trained to do the same. As a picture of an attitude to women which idolises them so long as they remain totally incapacitated for any independent activity, it has a comic/ironic force which can hardly have been unintended. Matilda does not drive home the subversive message but it is to be hoped that some at least of her readers would have seen the point.

Whatever readers made of it, *Dr Jacob* was and continued to be a success with readers. In 1898 Matilda proudly told a friend that ten thousand copies of the novel were sold every year in the United Kingdom and the colonies in cheap — "too cheap", she adds — editions.

In 1862, after Frankfurt Matilda went to Vienna. Every day a parade took place in which the Emperor rode accompanied by an entourage of all the highest and most fashionable of Viennese society, a spectacle which for brilliance and gaiety far outshone anything in London; but Matilda noted also the poverty in some areas and saw men and women living in conditions little if anything short of slavery. Nevertheless, she enjoyed her time in Vienna. She lived with a distinguished family and moved in privileged circles, and was delighted to find that she could go unaccompanied anywhere she chose, whether to popular restaurants or to a late performance at the opera. "Nowhere and under no circumstances could a young foreign girl enjoy greater freedom and safety", she writes, but the efficient policing which guaranteed her safety had its drawbacks. In some respects Vienna was far too well policed and it does not escape Matilda that Austrians never discussed politics "because speech no more than the press was free". She took note of such things but at this stage her attention was mainly absorbed by the passing show. Relatively trivial matters capture her attention and she passes on observations and anecdotes which add life and atmosphere to her accounts. She is shocked, for example, by the continental habit of dispensing with bedrooms. Even in rich Viennese households, she notes with amazement, the day rooms of the family were transformed into sleeping places at night and domestic servants slept on the floor wherever they could. Such things could never happen in even the poorest of Suffolk households, Matilda exclaims, for there everyone, ploughmen and dairymaids included, always had their bedrooms. The train of thought leads her to repeat a story of "that arch-despot and arch-voluptuary Louis XIV". The women of what she calls "his hareem" had no better conditions for their lying-in, she claims, than itinerant tinkers' wives: "In the very height of her ascendancy Louise de la Vallière was brought to bed in a landing or passage of general use. 'Pray be quick and bring the child into the world,' she groaned to her accoucheur; 'lots of people will be passing presently' ". "We English", Matilda concludes, "are a very boastful race ... I must aver, however, that the English nation may well be proud of two inventions — that of the bedchamber and of another smaller apartment, which shall here be nameless".

She was, she claims, naturally adventurous and fearless when she was young and confronted adventures "with the happiest unconcern, defiant of danger, no matter what shape it wore". What particular daring adventures she had in mind does not appear but certainly, especially in her later travels in France, she was always ready to brave discomfort and even on occasions some danger, in explorations which took her into remote areas rarely visited by foreigners or by the French themselves. One "adventure" which offered and which would have changed her whole life, Matilda baulked at. Still on her German travels, she was one day sightseeing in Munich when she unexpectedly ran into an acquaintance from Salzburg, "of the other sex", as she somewhat coyly describes him. He was a Hungarian patriot and he had, it appears, fallen in love with Matilda who, for her part, had not been entirely immune. "Exile shared with a victim of despotism can but wear an enticing aspect in the eyes of a romantic girl" she writes, "and", she adds, daringly, "foreign love-making has charms of its own". Yet she resists. While she ate black bread and cold sausage in the railway restaurant and drank a mug of beer, her lover poured out protestations "fervid as any ever poured into a maiden's ear", but her train was due and there was no time to talk or consider. "Prudence ... got the better of impulse" and she continued her journey — fancy-free, she claims, and dedicated to her vocation: "Instead of accepting Hungarian nationality and a home in the new world, I pursued a literary calling at home". This seems to have been the only direct proposal of marriage Matilda received (though probably not her only love affair) but she is careful to forestall any suggestion that she regretted rejecting it.

She writes more fully about another kind of proposal made to her about this time. This was an offer by a wealthy maiden lady to take her as her companion: "I had only to make myself agreeable and the best of everything material, horses, carriages, good dinners, foreign travel, were mine for the rest of my days." It was not uncommon for well-to-do unmarried or widowed ladies to seek company other than maid or courier and Miss Brown, as Matilda calls her, was amiable, well-bred, mildly interesting and had a handsome fortune. The offer did not tempt Matilda but it provoked an interesting episode with Amelia. Their individual travels had for once brought them to the same spot and they had met in Heidelberg where Matilda confided Miss Brown's offer to her older cousin. Amelia was adamant that she should not accept it: " 'Keep your freedom', she said. 'Return to Suffolk. Go your own way. Let that delightful' — I am not sure that she did not add another expletive beginning with the same letter — 'Let that delightful Miss Brown go!' " This sounds like a fully authentic episode and is not without its piquancy since, as Matilda points out, Amelia had herself accepted what to all appearances was a somewhat similar position for herself. In 1864, four years after her parents' death, Amelia left London and moved to Westbury-on-Trym, now an urban district within the orbit of Bristol but at that date a village. There she shared a home with a woman of about her mother's age, Mrs Ellen Braysher, an old family friend. Amelia's close attachment to her mother made her death a particularly grievous blow to her and the decision to share a home with Mrs Braysher was evidently motivated by need of another figure who could be in some sense a mother-substitute. Mrs Braysher and Amelia, thirty years apart in age, had known each other for a long time, were bound by common family reminiscences and by common experience of grief at the loss of beloved family members. They continued to live together in The Larches, Eastfield, till they died within a few months of each other, Mrs Braysher in February, Amelia in April 1892. Their situation had really nothing in common with that which Miss Brown proposed for Matilda but Amelia's warnings of the restraints and obligations of such a relationship indicate that she was alert to the pros and cons of her own decision to share her life with Mrs Braysher. Throughout their many years together she never failed in loyalty and affection to her elderly friend but the intensity of her relationship with her mother and the blow which she suffered at her death left scars on Amelia which Mrs Braysher could not heal. Nothing and no-one truly replaced the mother and this keenly felt loss reverberating throughout her life seems likely to have been, at least in part, responsible for her lonely ending. Ebullient as she had been in her youth, in her later years Amelia adopted a reclusive, quasi-monastic life at the service of the Egypt Exploration Society with only one contemporary, Kate Bradbury, as confidante and friend. Kate Bradbury remained with her to the end during last painful months of illness.

Meanwhile, if Matilda at any point hesitated over Miss Brown's offer, Amelia's advice as the older and more experienced cousin carried the day and, rejecting a patron as she had rejected a husband, Matilda committed herself finally to making her own way by her own resources. After Germany she spent some months in Paris, lodging with a Mlle Eugénie, who taught French language and literature, and her sister Josephine who was said to be a singing mistress but who appeared to have other resources, largely owing, it would seem, to the gentlemen who were frequent visitors. Mlle. Eugénie was a slightly deformed, ill-dressed and ill-kempt little person, "of a certain age". Her younger sister was "well proportioned and not absolutely ugly" and regarded herself as "a fairy, a veritable syren". Matilda's account draws on lively memory and is full of life and humour. The sisters were "At Home" on Thursdays and on these occasions Mlle Josephine would wear white, a choice which Matilda notes with some sceptical amusement. Of her admirers in regular attendance, the most devoted was a painter but it was plain to Matilda "that he no more dreamed of matrimony than of reaching the moon on a bicycle". Tolerant and entertained, far from censorious, Matilda knows very well what is going on. Eager collector of distinguished acquaintance as she became, Matilda had a warm and ready sympathy for the humbler and the less well-to-do, whether they were the country folk of her native Suffolk or, as here, the somewhat shabby, even seedy, society of proletarian Paris.

The story of Josephine and her admirers is an example of Matilda in her best raconteur mode, full of comedy and also of humanity. It speaks for her close familiarity with Paris life on a far from socially elevated level and it provides a background to the acerbic remarks she makes about French political life at the time. In these days of the Empire, in France as in Austria, no one dared to discuss politics or criticise the government. A "tinsel Caesar" held "dissolute state" at the Tuileries and under his repressive régime Matilda saw the seeds of the Commune to come. She cannot resist adding a footnote to her main story: "A public monument ought to be erected to the honour of Mr Frederic Harrison", she writes. Frederic Harrison was a prominent figure of the second half of the nineteenth century who became a close friend of Matilda's later years. The particular trigger of her approval on this occasion is that "largely due to his initiative and magnificent protest", the remains of the Prince Imperial, (Louis Napoleon's son) were not interred in Westminster Abbey, "in near proximity to the grave of our great Elizabeth". The young prince met a sad end, Harrison concedes, but France had no cause to weep for his death: "The Napoleonic legend had cost French fathers and mothers too dear". Dean Stanley, Matilda writes, "lost his temper about the matter" but Harrison's party won the day and the grave of "our great Elizabeth" remained uncontaminated by the intruder. The echoes of inflammatory speeches on this then burning topic and the warmth of enraged feelings aroused come clear off the page. The story is typical of the freewheeling, unsystematic manner of Matilda's reminiscences which makes the act of reading rather like reaching into a bran-tub, never knowing what amusing, illuminating or eccentric item will come to the surface next.

The foreign travel of her twenties came to an end in 1864 when Edward Edwards, Matilda's father, died. The big house at Westerfield had already been given up in favour of a smaller "occupation", the management of which now devolved on Matilda, together with one unmarried (and unnamed) sister. She consequently returned to Suffolk as Amelia advised. The practical responsibility added to her childhood experience gave her the grasp of rural and farming life which enabled her in later books to write with confidence and authority about farm practices and economics but her life as a "farmeress" did not last long, for the sister died in 1865 whereupon Matilda left rural life and based herself instead in London. This did not mean that she gave up travelling: far from it. In the same year she ventured well outside the usual tourist range, going to French North Africa on a visit which brought her acquaintance with Barbara Bodichon, née Leigh Smith, a vigorous proponent of women's rights and a future foundress of Girton College, Cambridge, friendship with whom was to be one of the most influential in Matilda's life. The visit to Algiers was overall as significant in its way as her visit to France would be a few years later for it brought her into contact with an intellectual, artistic and influential circle beyond any she had yet known. Through Barbara Bodichon she was introduced to the cream of Anglo-French society in Algiers and she gained entrée to a distinguished and cosmopolitan company back at home in England. The novels she had so far written drew heavily on her own experiences, as all her novels would continue to do, but the range was now to broaden out into areas which had so far been inaccessible to her. She had already in her travels in France and Germany come a long way, in every sense, from Suffolk and its farms and farmers but much wider horizons were now to open. In swiftly composed books, *A Winter with the Swallows* (1867) and *Through Spain to the Sahara* (1868), she recorded her immediate impressions. Later, in 1912, pulling together her memories of a long and active life, she worked over these books again, and added fresh material to them in a volume entitled *In French Africa*. She has as ever a sharp eye for the anecdote which, though it may be trivial in itself, gives the flavour of a scene, a personality or an event and her North African books like all her collections of reminiscences remain entertaining, even illuminating. The first visit was followed by a second in the next year. This in turn led, via Barbara Bodichon, to a week on the Isle of Wight with George Eliot and George Henry Lewes and thence to Matilda's mature career as prolific novelist and eager friend of France. The African experiences paved the way but Matilda cherished them in themselves. On her scale there could be no greater compliment than the one she pays at the conclusion of the 1912 volume when, in defiance of her many contemporaries (including her cousin) who succumbed to "the glamour cast by Italy", she declares that "could I once more undertake overseas travel I should forego that much-loved land, the France of '89, and a third time sail for her delightful shores of Barbary!"

Amelia Edwards as a young woman

Matilda Betham-Edwards as a young woman

Chapter Two

ALGERIA AND AFTER

The invitation to go to Algiers in the winter of 1866/7 came from an artist friend, Sophia, Lady Dunbar, who was herself visiting the country as a guest of the Governor-General's wife, Mme MacMahon, and was living in the splendour of the Vice-Imperial palace. Matilda understood that she was to be accommodated similarly but, perhaps because an untitled Miss Edwards, farmer and farmer's daughter, was several steps too far below the reach of such elevated patronage, things did not turn out like that. The friend was not at the quayside to meet the boat and Matilda endured a long, hot and uncomfortable wait before she finally arrived, bearing the news that instead of the grand quarters Matilda was expecting, she was to be put up in a hotel and, instead of being driven there by carriage, she was to walk. This reception was, to say the least, disconcerting for Matilda who had expected quite other treatment but the friend appeared unembarrassed. Matilda has little more to say of her but she had cause to be grateful after all, for it was through this lady that she was to receive invitations to Mme MacMahon's receptions and also to be introduced to the celebrated Barbara Bodichon in whose house, the friend promised, she would meet "all the best people, French and English, in the place". Mindful of this, Matilda chose not to indulge in ill-humour and recriminations. She solaced herself instead with the beauty of the country, the picturesque appearance of the people and the coming to life around her, so it seemed, of scenes from *The Arabian Nights* and the Bible. She was much impressed by the beauty of Arab men: "If human beings were made only to be looked at," she writes, "the sons of the desert assuredly bear the palm". An invitation to visit the Bodichon house duly arrived and Matilda set out for the large, straggling, Moorish-looking house on hills above the town where Barbara Bodichon and her French-Algerian doctor husband lived.

Barbara Bodichon, born Barbara Leigh-Smith, was nine years older than Matilda and a woman who, in spite of difference in wealth and social position, became a close friend of Matilda's and one to whom she offered unstinted admiration. Barbara was the daughter of Benjamin (Ben) Smith, an M.P. and a member of the powerful and ramifying Smith-Nightingale-Bonham-Carter group. His radical sympathies extended to his private life and Barbara and her four siblings were the children of Anne Longden, daughter of a corn miller in Derbyshire, with whom Ben lived openly though he did not marry her. Five children were born of whom Barbara was the eldest. As Leigh-Smiths (the Leigh came from an ancestress), they were given a first-class education and none seems to have suffered serious disadvantage from their illegitimacy. Certainly Barbara made an unquestioned place for herself as a prominent and effective figure in public life and she won recognition also as a talented artist. In distributing his money Ben Smith treated sons and daughters alike and Barbara in consequence was a wealthy woman. Together with his money she also inherited her father's strong sense of social responsibility and all her life was propelled by a desire to put her fortune at the service of the many good causes she espoused, education and women's rights prominent among them. She worked hard and effectively for all of them, the most substantial evidence of her endeavours being the existence of Girton College, Cambridge, of which she, with Emily Davies, was co-founder. She had initiative, enthusiasm, valuable contacts, money and, additional to all that, a very striking appearance with, in Matilda's words, "long sumptuous golden hair" and "Titianesque colouring".

On Matilda's first visit to Campagne du Pavillon, as the Bodichon house was called, Barbara was full of excitement over a book she was reading, the newly published letters and papers of Caroline Cornwallis, an earlier campaigner for universal education and equal rights for women. Barbara at once wanted to share her enthusiasm with the new guest and no doubt Matilda responded politely but Barbara's hopes for a dedicated fellow-worker in the cause of women's rights were then and later doomed to disappointment. Barbara tried from the first to enlist Matilda in her various campaigns but Matilda rejected her approaches. Her argument was the same one that she used in spurning her Hungarian suitor and that she would use time and again when pressed to give active support to causes with which she personally sympathised. Her first and overriding duty was to literature, she claimed, and she would allow nothing to deflect her from it. However much she enjoyed the Hungarian's "foreign love-making" and to whatever extent she sympathised with the causes Barbara cherished, she was determined to pursue her one chosen path. In later life she claimed this resolute fidelity to her pen as a badge of honour but a sensible recognition of practicalities may properly have been among her motives for rejecting an uncertain life with a Hungarian exile and also for refusing to involve herself too deeply in Barbara's projects. Barbara was cushioned against misadventure and the odium of public controversy by her status as a wealthy woman of good family. She could afford to pursue a challengingly unconventional path whereas Matilda had to make her own way in the world and had neither family nor money to fall back on. The books she wrote, though not explicitly propagandist, were to be her contribution to radical thinking, whether about the nature and role of women or about other aspects of the social structure but she would march behind no banners nor associate herself with any organisation. Her friendship with Barbara Bodichon came to be warm and valued on both sides but Matilda clung to her freedom of choice and of action.

In this she followed, deliberately or not, cousin Amelia's example for Amelia also kept aloof from active engagement with causes on which nevertheless she felt strongly. In an exceptional public exposure of her political sympathies, she was briefly in the 1850s a member of a radical group surrounding the painter Samuel Laurence but otherwise expression of her strong hostility to the existing social system has to be deduced from her novels. She signed John Stuart Mills's 1866 petition to Parliament for female suffrage but this was the limit of her public activity. On her death she left her Egyptological collection to University College, London, the first college to award degrees to men and women on equal terms, and she left her watercolours and personal papers to Somerville College, Oxford, a women's college, but these were private acts not public demonstrations. Like Matilda, she needed all her energies to carve out an independent life which would do justice to her gifts and in itself be witness to the personal and intellectual fitness of women for a full share in the nation's life. During her Peckham days Matilda had been a witness of the hesitations which had attended Amelia's choice of career and the lesson in focussing and concentration which followed, once choice had been made, was one sharp-eyed Matilda was not likely to miss.

In spite of Barbara's disappointment at her failure to recruit Matilda as an active supporter of her causes, friendship between the two developed rapidly and Matilda came to know both the Bodichons, husband and wife, well. Barbara divided her time between countries, summer in England, winter in Algiers, but her commitment to the welfare of Algeria and its ethnic mix was as wholehearted as was her husband's. Eugène Bodichon, French-Algerian by birth and doctor by profession, came from a family which numbered among them some who had gone to the guillotine but he himself was a committed republican and reformer. He had been a supporter of the July Revolution of 1830 which overthrew Charles X and the Bourbon dynasty and put Louis Philippe, "the citizen king", on the throne. Matilda would later on say that it was Bodichon's stories of recent French history and her admiration for him and his part in it which lit the flame of her henceforth lifelong devotion to France.

He brought his reformist ideas to Algeria when he settled there, instigating the liberation of slaves, championing the cause of the Berbers and in both his political and medical life working selflessly for Algeria and its people. Matilda gives him full credit and claims for him a place of honour in French and Algerian memory. She noted with satisfaction that husband and wife were equally indifferent to race, nationality, colour and creed but cared only to minister to those in need.

Living close to them and imbibing their influence, Matilda also took an enlightened view of the country and the people — but within obvious limits. She does not question France's right of occupation and stresses only the benefits that French conquest brings. There is implicit criticism of those among his countrymen who fall short when she stresses her admiration for the high standards Dr Bodichon sets, but that is as far as it goes. Even the position of Algerian women does not rouse her to protest though one or two domestic incidents she encounters are discomforting. The older Matilda is not by any means shy of expressing controversial opinions but, like the earlier books which it absorbs, *In French Africa* is a pleasant and unprovocative travel book, fluently written by an intelligent, alert observer with eyes and ears open to pick up whatever is to be seen and heard. She admires Islamic art and makes an effort to learn Arabic in order to read some of the literature. Unusually for her time and later, she also admires the religion. A ritual celebration involving frenzied dance and self-laceration is too much for European nerves and a bloody sacrifice of birds and goats is horrifying but she has great respect for some aspects of Ramadan. "Nothing in the Christian religion is more impressive than the ceremony of evening worship during Ramadan", she writes. She admires and respects Mohammed, reads the Koran and quotes from it frequently and it is borne in on her that judgements made in ignorance of the country and its people are useless: "One must live in Mohammedan countries to realize the inherent connection between Mohammed's religion and the people and country to whom he bequeathed it. One must study the Arabs, too, before talking of converting them to Christianity". These are far-sighted remarks, left undeveloped but remarkably open-minded in her time and not irrelevant later. Agreeable and even-tempered travelling companion as she is, some of her observations are challenging enough to keep contemporary readers alert and they retain rather more than muted historical interest now.

For any modern reader, however, the life of the book is likely to be in the anecdotes with which she enlivens it as she does all her non-fiction work. Two of her stories are connected with Dr Bodichon. One relates to an aunt of his, a young woman about to take her place in fashionable society, who rides one day to visit a sister of hers who is a cloistered nun. When the time comes to leave and the convent gates are opened for her, her horse backs away. She tries three times to urge him through but each time he refuses. "I recognise the voice of heaven!" cries the young lady, throwing the reins over the horse's head, and preparing to dismount. "My vocation is here"; and there she stays for the rest of her life. Given that in other works Matilda frequently and vehemently expresses hatred for Roman Catholicism and monasticism, it might have been expected that this story would disgust her but sheer narrative piquancy overrides prejudice and she allows herself to be entertained. An episode from Dr Bodichon's own life gives her another tale to tell. Bodichon was a keen lover of animals. He was also the possessor of a thick mop of hair. One night when he was bivouacking in the desert, a mouse crept into his hair and settled there. He was too kind-hearted to disturb the creature and left it until morning when he had to move — a humane gesture if, one might think, somewhat unhygienic. Matilda was delighted by the story. She herself, an ardent anti-vivisectionist, felt keenly on behalf of animals and in her later travels in France she deplored the insensitivity which she found a regrettable defect in French character. The French Dr Bodichon's care for the mouse was all the more to his personal credit.

In French Africa is a relaxed book largely made up of scenes and events of years before which had caught her attention at the time by their novelty or eccentricity. Some are very slight but not without charm, as when Mme MacMahon tries out her colloquial English at a formal reception and exclaims as new guests mount the staircase, "Ah! What a bother! There's a lot of people coming up". Young Matilda was amused also by stories of MacMahon himself and the taciturnity he was famed for, as on the occasion when he was surveying a disastrous flood near Toulouse and all he could manage was "Que de l'eau! Que de l'eau!" Reminiscences like these belong to a period of comparative innocence when Matilda in the '60s was sunning herself in viceregal society. A later day was to come when in 1870 MacMahon would be recalled to France and become second President of the Third Republic. Matilda was then to excoriate "the MacMahon tyranny", as she calls it, when "clericalism, militarism and the Napoleonic idea were rampant". In the 1860s in Algeria her political sensibilities were not so sharpened as they later became and her pleasure in introduction to viceregal society was foremost in her mind. Her attention was fully taken up by the here and now as she studied the unfamiliar scene and the people who acted in it.

Her horizons were further extended and her visit enlivened by Dr Bodichon's stories of his experiences as doctor and administrator, one such tale leading eventually to an acquaintance which gave Matilda particular delight. It concerned one Bombonnel, a Frenchman renowned in Algeria as a fearless panther hunter, who on one of his expeditions had been savagely attacked by the prey he was stalking. His jaw was broken and he lost nose and teeth but Eugène Bodichon attended him, mended his face as best he could and made him at least presentable. The story interested Matilda and when in the summer of 1879 she met Bombonnel himself in France she eagerly pursued the acquaintance. They used to walk together through the woods near Dijon where he had settled in later life and he told her how when he was young he had gone to the New World, hawked shoes and stockings in the streets of New Orleans, traded with Indian tribes and fallen in love with a beautiful Indian girl. Returning to Europe in 1841 he had married and then begun his career as panther-hunter, returning every winter to Algiers and there accumulating fame and fortune. When the Franco-Prussian war broke out he became an effective and ruthless franc-tireur [an irregular soldier, a guerilla] who won the admiration of Victor Hugo.

Matilda quotes extensively from his own written account of his panther-hunting adventures in *In French Africa* and she draws also on the war-time stories he told her in their walks together. She had from childhood on been an insatiable observer of people and behaviour and all her life she collected specimens, as a lepidopterist collects butterflies. Bombonnel was a treasure amongst them adding a touch of the violent and the exotic to her range of varieties of human behaviour. His adventures appealed to her for their derring-do and for their pungency and she tells and retells his story several times. Recycling became a feature of her work when new material failed to keep pace with output but economy is not the only motive at work here. The strongly-spiced life of this man, who was on occasion a cold-blooded killer of fellow men as well as of animals —"c'est la guerre", he said — and who was also a sympathetic and knowledgeable lover of the natural world, made a great appeal to her by its rarity. Bombonnel was a man dedicated to risk-taking and perhaps in a sense Matilda envied him, pulled as she was between self-defining pursuit of her individual path and a prudent awareness of the risks of going too far. However that may be, she counts Bombonnel as one of the major prizes of her stay in Algeria and he keeps an honoured place alongside the literary and political and otherwise distinguished characters whom she delights to observe and record.

A second visit to North Africa followed in 1867/8, this time at Barbara Bodichon's personal invitation. She and Matilda travelled through France and Spain calling at sites of interest on the way and, Barbara Bodichon being what she was, these sites inevitably included schools, lunatic asylums and prisons. They were to land at Oran, and loop round through Mascara and Relizane back to Algiers. From

Mascara they made a brief visit to Saida, "the threshold of the Sahara" Matilda calls it, where she smelt "the sweet air of the desert". The distances were not great by modern standards but today's travellers fretting at inefficient railways, traffic congestion in cities, security checks at airports and other inconveniences may marvel at the patience, hardiness and sheer determination of women from a generation commonly thought of as cosseted and over-protected. Delayed in their efforts to get to Gibraltar, and forced to put up in Algeciras, they are accommodated in "an insectivorous hole of a room" devoid of anything but two poor beds and innumerable fleas. The French communities in Africa are havens of civilisation but, though tempted to stay, Matilda and Barbara press on, undaunted by the need at times for a military escort through areas threatened by marauding Arabs. Nor are they deterred by primitive travelling conditions; a whole day, for instance, in a rickety carriage with unglazed windows when, in addition to the discomfort of the seating, they suffer alternately from burning sun and the fierce wind. They see something of a plague of locusts, they pass through districts ravaged by malaria, and they see with distress the immediate consequences of an earthquake: "One must tread on the heels of an earthquake to understand what it is — the suddenness of it, the despair of it, the desolation of it". Some danger and considerable physical discomfort attended these journeys, but Matilda and Barbara were undoubtedly privileged persons, protected at all points by their money and their nationality and with the leisure to sketch and to enthuse about the landscape and the flowers which were a special source of pleasure to Matilda.

To her credit Matilda not only observes but feels and associates herself with the deprivations and suffering of the native people. During their bone-shaking, skin-scorching journey in the derelict carriage, she and Barbara come upon an Arab settlement and make friends with a Bedouin family. There is nothing patronising in this as Matilda describes it. On the contrary she has great respect for the grandmother and she grieves sincerely for the small mite stricken with malaria. Arabs were too poor to buy quinine and Matilda knows that the small bottle she has with her and which she leaves for the child will not be enough to save him. When in 1912 she looks back on Algeria with longing and calls it her El Dorado, it is as " a holiday ground" that she is thinking of it, a place with "the charm of witchery" beyond any other of the many beautiful places she has seen. The political and economic situation which underlay the sights and scenes so delightful to visiting Europeans is not then in her mind but she has not been blind to it. *In French Africa* notably eschews the superiority and condescension which disfigure many accounts of alien lands and for that as for its other qualities as a travel book it stands to her credit.

One episode during the 1867/8 visit is of particular interest in itself and also because it gives impetus to a line of thought which is to be conspicuous in novels which follow, particularly *The Sylvestres* of 1871. Matilda and Barbara hear that a Fourierist colony, or phalanstery, has been established somewhere in the neighbourhood of Oran and they determine to visit it. Charles Fourier (1772-1837) was a French socialist thinker who envisaged a new order of society in which the interests of the community as a whole could be safeguarded without sacrifice of individual choice and individual talent. In this society all members would share equally in the work necessary to maintain the community and all without exclusion would share in its intellectual and aesthetic pleasures. Fourierist ideas had a considerable following in England in mid-century, as in the group around Samuel Laurence to which cousin Amelia was for a time attached. Sadly, when Matilda and Barbara arrive at the site of the Algerian phalanstery it has vanished without trace. Only one couple remain of the original settlement and Fourier and his ideals have long ceased to mean anything to them. Apart from these two, there are otherwise on the site only "ordinary French labourers working after the ordinary way". The experiment in socialist living has failed but Matilda refuses to be utterly downcast. Reflecting afterwards on what she has seen she concludes that the experiment and the ideals which activated it had not been in vain. The ideal community had crumbled under the strain of practical implementation but the dreams of Fourier and those who thought like him had had effect all the same. In England she finds their influence in the establishment of such things as free libraries, garden suburbs and university extension lectures. Concepts of moral and social duty have, she believes, been strengthened by the idealism of the Fourierists and through them and their like "that grand social watchword — solidarity" has entered the national vocabulary. *The Sylvestres*, in its turbulent enactment of the pros and cons of Fourierism, is ample evidence of the impact Fourier's ideas made on her.

The friendship between Matilda and Barbara Bodichon was close but there was nevertheless a great disparity between their social positions, one a woman who could draw on family affluence and influence to further her many energetic activities and the other a farmer's daughter, nine years younger, who was to all intents and purposes living on her wits. Matilda was proud and gratified to be a member of the Bodichon circle and for her part Barbara was pleased with Matilda's liveliness and intelligence and described her to a correspondent as "a clever, cheerful, vigorous-minded person". It could hardly be a friendship of equals but Barbara felt confident enough in the acceptability of Matilda's personality and talents to extend to her on their return the privilege of introduction to a friend of long standing who was close in a way Matilda could not be, the great George Eliot.

The friendship between Barbara Bodichon and George Eliot was of long standing and George Eliot's illicit relation with G. H. Lewes had had no power to interrupt it. Matilda herself was evidently relaxed on that score. As a novelist dependent on wide sales she learned that heroines had to be "pure", "sweet" and utterly without sexuality, though she tried to give them some independent spirit, but as a woman of the world she took a tolerant view, fully aware, no doubt, of the loss she herself would suffer if cut off from the society of two of the most eminent women of the day and the circle surrounding them. Back from her winter in Algiers, in early summer 1868, Barbara hastened at once to call on "Marian" who was at that time living at The Priory, St John's Wood. She took Matilda with her but permission to meet the great woman was not to be taken for granted and Matilda had to wait outside till Barbara called from the doorway to say she might enter.

There could hardly have been a more striking contrast in appearance than that between the two women who then greeted her, Barbara Bodichon with her bright hair and blue eyes, her whole person radiating vitality, and George Eliot "with her large sallow features lighted up by intermittent flashes of thought or feeling, her angular, somewhat stooping figure, stiffly habited in black, the whole forming a sombre Rembrandt-like figure". To Matilda she was awe-inspiring and unforgettable. Some found her ugly but Matilda records how Frederick Leighton with his artist's eyes saw differently. "How beautiful she is!" he exclaimed in one of the famous Sunday afternoon At Homes at The Priory to which Matilda, having been judged acceptable, was given entrée. She thought he was right and agreed that spiritual beauty and inner radiance counted for more than flawless features.

Admission to gatherings at The Priory was a bonus of friendship with Barbara Bodichon. It was there that Matilda began to build up her roll-call of eminent acquaintances, though she was too insecure and inexperienced at first to make as much as she would have liked of these initial contacts. She observed Browning and did not like him. She had always, she says, considered him "a poet immensely inferior to his glorious wife" and now she finds it difficult to believe "that the hero of 'Sonnets from the Portuguese' and the elderly flirt and chatterer of nonsense" she observes in George Eliot's drawing room could be one and the same person. The "colossal figure of Turgeneff" once appeared but Matilda had to be content with noting his "air of vague, quiet, dreamy sadness" for she had no conversation with him. The company in general was somewhat overpowering to her at this time when life on the Suffolk farm was still not far behind her and she had as yet made only first steps towards making a career and a name. She was particularly disconcerted when Lewes brought over Liebreich, famous for having been the first to make use of chloral, and to her dismay Lewes left them to talk. She had enough German after her many months spent at Stuttgart and Frankfurt but "a tête à tête with a scientist" was a daunting challenge. However, as she put it, he tried to talk down to her and she tried to talk up to him, until relief came with the arrival of tea. The new milieu threw up other awkward moments which had to be negotiated as well as might be but acquaintance with Mme Bodichon was rapidly expanding Matilda's social range.

Through her Matilda came to meet Edwin (later Sir Edwin) Chadwick and on one occasion in 1865 she accompanied him and his wife on an inspection of the Poor Law School at Southall. Lord John Russell, Liberal politician and reformer, who had assisted in drafting the first Reform Bill of 1832 and who steered it through Parliament, was also of the party. Chadwick had devoted himself to Poor Law reform and to public health, especially sanitation. He was responsible for supervising the construction of an effective sewage disposal system and Matilda records a contemporary jibe that in old age and senility he would be haunted by visions of himself transformed into a monster drain-pipe spreading throughout the entire kingdom. In 1865 he was "a stalwart middle-class gentleman in his prime", a striking physical contrast to Lord John, "an undersized elderly scion of as noble and historic family as any in England". She was proud to have been brought into this company and in old age she records the episode with pleasure but is impatient with her youthful shyness. Experience had taught her a lesson which she diligently applied, that those who aim to make a mark in the world should never be backward in coming forward. "I never venture to compliment my betters", she says, but, back in 1865:

> might not a word or two as to Lord John's achievements in belles-lettres from an accredited authoress have here afforded pleasure? How aptly would come in, say, a quotation from one of his twenty works, above all from his romances and two tragedies!

This reads comically as over-valuation of a compliment from a young woman Lord John had probably previously never heard of. Behind it is the retrospective frustration of the older woman who has learnt never to squander an opportunity to draw the attention of persons of importance and influence. She has the consolation, however, of knowing that at least one of her later books about France does become known to Lord John, since in one of his own works he quotes from it.

Between 1868 and 1871 Matilda was living at Abingdon Villas in Kensington, which was then a quaint, old-world district still with something rural about it. It was from there that she made forays to George Eliot's conversaziones, to Madame Bodichon's cosmopolitan gatherings and to Lord Houghton's celebrated breakfasts. It was said of Richard Monckton Milnes (as he was before he became Baron Houghton) that he knew everybody worth knowing at home and abroad and it was certainly a mark of distinction to be included in such company. She had an inexhaustible passion for material to flesh out the studies of life and manners which she meant her novels to be and she eagerly cultivated acquaintance with the eminent in the artistic and intellectual worlds. It was not celebrity itself which attracted her, much less money, but those minds which were prepared to think beyond the pale of convention and challenge outworn ideas.

Prejudice and intolerance at all times deeply offended her. At one of Barbara Bodichon's gatherings she met a distinguished mathematician who, because he was a Jew, was debarred from the academic honours which were his due. Matilda was indignant on his behalf at the time and linked his story with that of another victim of contemporary intolerance, the crusading social reformer and determined secularist, Charles Bradlaugh. Bradlaugh's triumph was to come later in 1886 when he took his seat as a member of the House of Commons, having successfully asserted his right to affirm his allegiance rather than take an oath by a God he did not believe in. Matilda's revulsion against the prejudices of impermeable conservatism was as active in the 1860s when she mixed with the celebrated in the Bodichon salon as it was twenty years later and as it remained to the end of her life.

One evening in September 1864, she climbed the narrow staircase behind a small shop in Holborn and entered a dingy, though well-lighted room where the first meeting was about to take place of what became the First International and was then known as the International Working Man's Association. Matilda had been brought there by a friend, Mr Cowell Stepney, a long-standing sympathiser with the cause. Karl Marx in person presided. Matilda, it goes without saying, made an eager survey of the company. Most of those present, she observed, were foreign: "all looked more or less worn out with the day's labour, whilst some were terribly attenuated and sallow". Marx himself much impressed her: "the portly, commanding frame, the powerful head with its shock of raven black hair, the imperturbable features, and slow measured speech, once seen and heard could never be forgotten." Fourier and Marx were of a different stamp but both represented socialism and socialism in one form or another Matilda looked upon as the beckoning future of a reformed society. Some twenty-five years after the Holborn meeting she was telling an acquaintance that socialism is the future of the world.

Matilda's story of Marx and the Marxist meeting was received with keen interest when she recounted it a few years later to George Eliot, George Henry Lewes and Barbara Bodichon. Barbara Bodichon had taken a house in Ryde on the Isle of Wight for the winter of 1870 and she invited Matilda to join her. George Eliot and George Henry Lewes were to be fellow-guests for Christmas. It was a memorable week for Matilda but it was a bleak time in the history of France with the Franco-Prussian war at its height and disasters for the cause of reform to follow. Events across the Channel weighed on the spirits of all of them. "We will come and weep with you over the sorrows of France", George Eliot promised her hostess, hardly a prospect to cheer a Yuletide gathering. Closer to home, the weather on the island was correspondingly unusually severe but Lewes (though sometimes blue with cold) did his best to cheer things up though his idea of jollity seems less than hilarious. At Christmas dinner the maidservant brought in an extra-large covered dish and Lewes explained to his hostess, Barbara, that he had taken the liberty of adding a special delicacy to the menu. The cover was removed and something which looked like a snake was revealed, uncoiling itself there. The "snake" was, in fact, the scourge with which the High Church clergyman from whom the house was rented used to mortify himself, a scarcely less agreeable appearance at the dinner-table than the snake itself would have been, even if it was not "stained with blood" as Matilda later, somewhat gratuitously, added. Whether, when they had managed to compose themselves, the company laughed heartily as at a good joke she does not record. She remembers the episode all her life and uses it in *In French Africa* as a sharp reminder that religious excesses are not confined to other races: "Well, after all that is said and done, are not cilices and scourges seen to-day in our own High Church vicarages?"

The combination of deep seriousness in George Eliot and Lewes's high spirits fascinated Matilda — it came as a shock to her when she first heard him address George Eliot as "Polly" but she was touched to hear George Eliot for her part call him "dear little man". It was with Lewes, in fact, that she spent most of her time, since George Eliot tended to pair off with Barbara Bodichon and Matilda and Lewes would walk and talk together. She found him a congenial and friendly companion and, moreover, he did her a great service. He wrote to Baron Tauchnitz and arranged for Matilda to meet him in person on her next visit to Germany, which was planned to take place shortly. The result of that introduction was that from that time onwards Matilda's novels were published in the Tauchnitz series thereby assuring her of a big continental market and adding considerably to her status and profit. The stay in the Isle of Wight under the same roof and in close company with George Eliot and Lewes was in every way a major prize in Matilda's social and professional life and not surprisingly she reverts to it more than once in her autobiographical writing. The accounts differ in minor detail but the main outlines remain constant.

Relations with George Eliot were more distant than those with Lewes appear to have been. The humble junior novelist had received some endorsement from the "grande dame" after the first meeting at her house when, as Barbara Bodichon reported to her, George Eliot had congratulated her on "possessing a friend who is without fringes", a somewhat obscure recommendation. Matilda took "fringes" to be fads and presumably George Eliot meant to commend her for being without affectation or trying eccentricities. Matilda was duly grateful for a word of approval from such a source, even if only a negative one but: "How much more gratified should I have been had she expressed her pleasure at meeting the authoress of such and such a novel!" she exclaims. She excuses George Eliot's "reticence" on the grounds of the impracticality of giving personal encouragement to every "youthful tyro". It may have been so but George Eliot may have read none of her books. If she had read *Kitty* she might indeed have had a word of encouragement to give.

Kitty, published in 1869, is the book which gave Matilda a place at Lord Houghton's table. It was, he declared, the best novel he had ever read and it is certainly Matilda's best, not excepting *The Lord of the Harvest*, the best known of the novels which come at the end of her novel-writing career and which draw on her memories of Suffolk life when she was a girl. *Kitty* is without doubt a good novel. A single driving impulse animates it throughout giving consistency and conviction to characters and narrative, qualities often missing from later novels where initial situations fail to develop and instead give way to plot entanglements and the doings of stock characters. There is no danger of this in *Kitty* for the subject here is one of which Matilda has thorough mastery. Kitty is a young woman who, as an orphan of questionable parentage, is adopted in infancy and brought up in a slatternly household in Fulham. The actual address is given — No. 3 Paradise Place — which seems to indicate an autobiographical connection of some kind but Paradise Place is otherwise unknown in Matilda's life story. In the novel it is at the heart of a north London bohemia frequented by impoverished artists and others whose tastes and talents are not matched by the state of their finances. Over it presides Polly Cornford, widowed, middle-aged, florid, untidy, ungrammatical, but with hand and heart open to all who need her. As well as adopting Kitty she has taken under her wing Perugino, otherwise known as Perry, who, when the story opens, is a young man a few years older than Kitty and deeply in love with her. He is an artist and as his name forecasts, incipiently a genius. Two young nieces who would otherwise be uncared for complete an unruly, disorganised household supported only by the occasional sale of Perry's pictures and the undervalued work of Mrs Cornford who is herself an artist of talent. It is a shabby, hand-to-mouth sort of life but abounding in vitality, warmth and, for the sunny Perry, it is full of hope. Kitty on the other hand, is sulky, dissatisfied and resentful that she was not born into what Matilda ironically refers to as "the kingdom of gentility". She determines to better herself, by which she means acquiring money and social position, but a career is out of the question and as a woman she can attain her goals only by attaching herself to someone who can give her what she craves. The novel charts the course of her successive attempts to climb the social ladder rung by rung. Her first move is to insert herself into the family of serious, quiet Dr Norman and her assiduous services to him and his children so endear her that he falls in love and asks her to marry him. She accepts him but then a better prospect offers and, deserting Norman, she goes to live as friend/companion to a wealthy widow. This life brings her luxury and a more sophisticated company which she enjoys but before long another offer beckons and she transfers her allegiance to the delicate daughter of a baronet. Each of her steps raises her higher in the social scale and she prides herself on having risen out of the chaotic and shabby life of Paradise Place. When the widowed baronet proposes and she becomes Lady Bartelotte she finally achieves a height which is beyond even her early ambitions.

Kitty has triumphed but she has also ruined herself. She has played her game brilliantly but it was never worth the candle and at the end her winnings consist of a dull and constrained existence with a miserly and boring husband in which she, who has shown herself to be a woman of extraordinary resource and personality, is valued mainly as the potential mother of an heir. This is not, however, a straightforward story of misplaced ambition in which wrong-doing Kitty gets her just desserts. From start to finish Matilda has great sympathy with her heroine and her urge to make a life for herself. It is true that Kitty is a mid-Victorian Becky Sharp, without the blatant sexual adventurism of Thackeray's heroine but exploiting her feminine wiles for their money value all the same, and it is no less true that the society whose acceptance she longs for is no more than Vanity Fair, a hollow world compared with the shabby but generous life of Paradise Place. Matilda enters nonetheless into Kitty's situation and the course it leads her to. Poor and alone as she is, is she to be blamed for thirsting for the prizes society offers, Matilda asks? Is she any more to be blamed because she uses the only skills she has, in order to advance herself in a world where birth and wealth override every other claim? To whatever degree the inequities and iniquities of society play a role in her story, however, Matilda is clear that Kitty's life-choices lie ultimately with Kitty and only with her: she alone must bear "the unspeakable responsibility of her own individual ego". It is a fine phrase and one which resonates with its relevance to Matilda herself. Matilda, like Kitty, started life without resources except ambition and natural gifts and she fully understands how a young woman could be driven by the compulsions of her nature to strive to make a mark in the world. She can also see how such energies might well lead not to fulfilment but to disaster. The underlying affinity between author and heroine contributes largely to the book's depth and subtlety as Matilda blends ironic observation, sympathetic feeling, scenes of comedy and scenes of disillusion into a firmly structured and convincing whole which is impressive evidence of her novelistic skills at their height. She was to write many more novels, most of which have their points of interest and their writerly merits, but *Kitty* is a *non-pareil*. It ranges widely up and down the social scale, from the denizens of a north London bohemia to the *beau monde* of Paris and the owners of title and country estate in affluent England. By the age of thirty-three Matilda had built up a substantial portfolio of varying types and temperaments in their native settings. She had come from an obscure life to a position in which she consorted with the great, the good and the not-so-good, looking always for the distinguishing trait or achievement which marked them out as in one way or another interesting. Her early life had taught her that such characters are not confined to the privileged classes and she certainly did not meet Polly Cornford in fashionable salons. Lord Houghton was piqued with curiosity to know where she had found this staunch, admirable and down-to-earth woman. The answer could be "anywhere in her travels at home and abroad" but the prototype was in all probability the full-flavoured, strong-natured country women of Suffolk whom Matilda always admired. She wrote about them in the late Suffolk novels and Mrs Brindle, in the novel *Half-Way* (1888) comes from the same family tree. Mrs Cornford with her grainy common sense and whimsical humour is of similar stock. Both of them add immeasurably to the novels in which they appear.

Matilda entertained her hostess and fellow-guests in Ryde with her account of Marx and his followers but she refrained from regaling them with description of another meeting addressed by another enthusiast for reform. The occasion this time was the first great public meeting arranged in support of women's suffrage and John Stuart Mill, a powerful advocate of the women's cause, was the speaker. In 1866 he presented a petition to Parliament on their behalf which Matilda at that time signed, as did cousin Amelia, and in 1869 he published his challenging essay *On the Subjection of Women*. The first meeting was a big occasion and Mill himself was impressive, as Marx was, but to Matilda's eyes there was something inexorable and rigid about Mill which, though awe-inspiring, made her uneasy:

> You felt as you gazed that chance and destiny, inclination and human weakness exercised no sway whatever over this man, that here were the immovable purpose, iron will and unflinching self-oblivion of which, for good or for evil, the world's umpires and leaders are made.

Surprisingly for one who usually remembered so much, she could not recall anything Mill said. She seems to have felt more humanity in Marx although later she hears evidence of Mill's "tender affection and delicate kindness" and acknowledges that she may earlier have misjudged him. In 1888 she visited his grave in Avignon and left flowers there in tribute to "the noble apostle of liberty".

Looking back on the week in Ryde and on all the period of her acquaintance with George Eliot, Matilda never pretended that she had been on intimate terms with her. She had noted with something like awe the way the heavy features could on occasions light up and become luminous, she had heard her play Beethoven at the piano — "perhaps somewhat too painstakingly" — seen her moved to rapture by a beautiful flower and recognised the sensitivity which caused her great distress if she thought she had been the cause of even the slightest pain to others, but George Eliot lived on a different plane. "On her shoulders seemed to rest the material and spiritual burdens of the universe". Matilda found her company oppressive. Writing of her nearly thirty years later in *Reminiscences*, she remembers that when George Eliot and Lewes departed from Ryde, the French painter Claude Daubigny took their place as house-guest. Anxious as he was about what was happening in his country and concerned for the personal safety of relatives and friends, nevertheless his company was a welcome relief: "Must I admit the fact? We were gayer, conversation was easier, existence more buoyant". Matilda rescinds nothing, however, of her admiration for George Eliot's intellectual supremacy. If she had not been a novelist, she believes, she might have been "a great woman-philosopher, Kant or Spencer of the other sex. That mighty intellect and commanding spirit would have silenced boyish supporters of male supremacy anyhow". (Perhaps she had one particular "boyish supporter" in mind.) She singles out *Middlemarch* as "an unanswerable argument against the asserters of unisexual intellectuality" but, great as that "prose epic" is, she finds its view of life dispiriting. *Middlemarch*, published in 1871-2, belongs to the period when Matilda knew her and in the woman herself, as in the tone of her later novels, she found a deep-seated melancholy: "the author and her books were steeped in sadness, not the hard, revolting pessimism of an Ibsen, a Flaubert, rather the tearful, pious sympathy of a Saint Francis d'Assisi or a Saint Theresa". For her part Matilda, vigorous and unquenchably eager for every detail of the passing show, rebels against the gloom even while she respects the mind. She came to think ever more firmly that George Eliot's intellectual capacity seriously disadvantaged her as a novelist. "George Eliot's sombre realism repels me", she said, "whilst I fully admit her enormous power". In a talk on Dickens given in Hastings in 1909 she contrasts Dickens's power to "exhilarate" with what she sees as a crushing over-intellectualisation apparent even in George Eliot's earlier novels.

Matilda was disappointed and exasperated by the marriage to John Cross after Lewes's death. Writing to Frederic Harrison in a letter of 1912, she comments that George Eliot "missed her chance of being a great Teacher by becoming Mary Ann Cross. Thus a noble life ending in an unnecessary bowing down to conventionality". After George Eliot's death Cross visited Matilda in Hastings where she was then living and she reports that she found him looking "younger than ever!"

The relationship between Matilda and Barbara Bodichon was closer in every respect than that between Matilda and George Eliot could ever be, despite Matilda's refusal to campaign alongside her friend and despite, also, the difference in their social standing. When Barbara's passionate giving of herself to all her causes led to a series of strokes and she died in 1891, leaving a bequest of one hundred pounds to Matilda, Matilda writes with real feeling of a woman who radiated vitality and the warmth of a generous spirit. To know her had indeed been a liberal education for Matilda, both by what she was in herself and by introducing her to some of the most interesting and eminent people of the day. Matilda acknowledged her debt with heartfelt gratitude. She had no intention of following in Barbara's footsteps, however. Barbara had been a talented artist but social causes had always taken precedence over a possible artistic career and as a consequence she had forfeited the renown as an eminent water-colourist which Matilda believed might have been hers had she concentrated her energies rather than widely distributing them. Matilda, on the contrary, would stick to her last as a professional writer and allow no deviation from it. It is ironic that having firmly resisted Barbara's attempts to persuade her to become an active champion of the cause of women, she was so far influenced by

Barbara's husband Dr Bodichon, and the conversations she had with him in Algiers, as to take up a cause of her own: the promotion of friendship and understanding between France and England. She could claim that her dedication to literature remained undiminished, since she put her writer's gifts at the service of France, but her suspicion of the baleful effect of a cause on an ambitious career were in large degree justified. She attained a measure of success in both her fields and her work for France was acknowledged but distinction as a novelist eluded her. In spite of her intentions, she allowed her attention to be distracted by divided interests even as she thought Barbara Bodichon's had been.

The cold winter weather that turned Lewes blue in 1870 made Matilda ill. On her return to London and "her little house at the back of Kensington High Street", she suffered a severe bronchial attack and was ordered to take a Mediterranean cruise. She promptly set off with a friend, sailing from Portsmouth to Gibraltar and afterwards to Malta, Alexandria, Athens, Venice and Cairo but health problems evidently persisted for some time. The bronchial problem may have been a particular worry. Cousin Amelia was to die in 1892 of acute bronchitis and inflammation of the lung at the age of sixty-one and Thomas Edwards, her father, had also died of bronchitis. Chest weakness may have run in the Edwards family and accounted for the several premature deaths which occurred among Matilda's brothers and sisters. George Eliot heard a report that Matilda was showing consumptive symptoms and remarks in a letter of 1874 that she is in a bad way and taking chloral — perhaps as she did so she remembered her uncomfortable conversation with Liebreich at a George Eliot salon! A year later the trouble has cleared up and she has, as George Eliot puts it, "got into the right groove". She adds that it is a pity that Matilda took up writing but she seems to be thinking rather of the possible strain on health than making a literary criticism.

The warm spring weather in the Mediterranean helped Matilda to recuperate and by midsummer she was in Leipzig intending to study music and German. Her accommodation turned out to be unexpectedly spartan and the weather cold and wet but Lewes had been as good as his word and given her an introduction to Baron Tauchnitz and, eager as always to widen her acquaintance, she became friendly with the family. Her first book to be published by the firm was *The Sylvestres* in 1871 and after that her novels were regularly reprinted by him and made available to a continental market. She profited considerably from his good offices as she gratefully acknowledged though she added, in complacent old age, that the benefit was not one-sided since her books would be "not without amusement and instruction to Continental readers". She is keen to repudiate any suggestion that Tauchnitz was not so much a lover of books as a shrewd businessman. He was a man of taste, she urges, who exercised his power for good and if "claptrap and balderdash" found their way into his series, the blame, she says, lay with the English public who bought such stuff, not with the publisher who produced it. She draws special attention to his generosity. In years before Anglo-American copyright existed, British authors, Dickens amongst them, complained bitterly that they were being robbed of their proper earnings by the transatlantic publishers who printed their works without payment. Matilda claims that she did not join this chorus because, after all, the Americans were doing nothing at that time illegal and the authors had the satisfaction of gaining an enormously enlarged readership. In any event, she claims it as a virtue of Tauchnitz that he acted as though international copyright were already in force and paid all his authors accordingly. His authors were duly grateful, to judge by the autograph letters which she saw in the Baron's library on a second visit in 1880 when she stayed in the Tauchnitz home. Thackeray in particular was pithy and to the point. "Don't be afraid of your English", he wrote, "a letter containing £.s.d. is always in pretty style".

Lewes and George Eliot had opened the doors of literary Leipzig for her but on her first visit she left after eight cold and rainy days. Smallpox broke out in the area and she moved on to Weimar, "the little Athens on the Ilm". Descendants of great figures of the not-so-distant past lived there still and Matilda, bearing "a satchel of letters introductory" made her choice. Ottilie von Goethe, Goethe's daughter-in-law, was then living in a modest flat and there Matilda sought her out, "an old lady dressed with scrupulous neatness, one might almost say coquetry". She was handsome still though there was a heaviness about the lower part of her face which Matilda judged to indicate a strong will. Her manners were courtly and she had the air of a great lady but, Matilda thought, no "intellectual force". She was much interested in higher education for women and listened attentively to what Matilda had to tell her about Barbara Bodichon's Girton scheme. Matilda herself was less enthusiastic about university education for women, fearing that it would suppress individuality and that the great names she admired, "the glorious galaxy of Victorian women", as she calls them, Charlotte Brontë, Elizabeth Barrett Browning and George Eliot, would have little to gain and might lose much from being put through the academic mill. No doubt she suppressed her misgivings on this occasion and reported fairly on Barbara Bodichon's ambitions for Girton. It was a remarkable experience to be in company with a woman who had known Goethe intimately and who, in recalling the past, would lapse into German and be able naturally to say "Der Vater sagte dies, der Vater meinte das" (my father said this, my father thought that). Frau von Goethe moved into

Goethe's house while Matilda was still in Weimar and she was invited to an evening gathering where she also met the elder son. He was amiable and conversable but struck her as a man whose life had been a failure. The overshadowing might of the Goethe name, she suspected, had inhibited the development of an individual and independent career and life had little relish for him.

After Goethe came Liszt. The landlady where Matilda was staying kept a table at midday at which friends and lodgers would meet and over their meal discuss knowledgeably and perceptively music and art and drama and other such topics; not, Matilda remarks, the standard of talk likely to be found under the roof of English landladies. One day a new figure appears, "an elderly priest, tall, almost Herculean in stature, and spare to lankness". His long silver hair frames a face "wearing a strange look only to be expressed by the word illumination, his eyes of diamond-like piercingness and brilliance"; but it is his long, restless hand which particularly catches Matilda's attention. It comes as something of a shock to her to learn that this is Liszt for, in the many years since he was last in London, England had forgotten him. It was very different in Weimar. As director of the opera and of concerts since 1849 and as composer and teacher he had made Weimar the musical centre of Germany and, though he had resigned his appointment in 1861, among his pupils and followers he was still the great luminary who followed Goethe as the brightest star in the sky. Matilda overheard him playing in her hotel one day and she longed to be invited to one of the Sunday afternoon parties held in his villa when, so it was said, he played Beethoven as no one had ever played Beethoven before. Matilda herself was taking piano lessons at the time with a Fraulein Constance, a young woman of about twenty-five who was a devotee of Liszt and Constance, it turned out, was easily able to get the desired invitation. So one Sunday Matilda heard him play, first on the organ of a little Catholic church close to his villa, and later in the house on his own piano when he performed an improvisation which was in effect a composition, "a sublime musical whole". Matilda was not one to let an opportunity slip when a star spun into her orbit and on this Sunday afternoon, while all were held spell-bound after the music ceased, she broke the silence by going boldly over to the pianist and assuring him, "Ah, Monsieur l'Abbée, vous nous avez transportés dans le Paradis!" whereupon he clasped her hands to his heart. She refrained from presenting herself as a fellow-musician, though from Peckham days onwards she had studied music, but she did take care that evening to establish her literary credentials by writing him a poem, a neat, well-turned little "Improvisation on Improvisation".

Acquaintance flourished when young Fraulein Constance arranged a picnic which Liszt attended and at which he was charming, enjoying common pleasures "as if he had been an ordinary mortal". He gave Matilda his arm as they strolled around the park and they talked together pleasantly; but when the time came to leave she had a reminder of that "perilous dower of fatal fascination" which she ascribed to cousin Amelia and which Liszt possessed in abundance. Matilda had already been disgusted by the shameless efforts of a middle-aged woman in the hotel to engage his attention. Now a group of girls was waiting for him just outside the park gate and as he alighted from the carriage they mobbed him, catching at his hands and kissing them. Another bevy would be waiting for him at his house door and Matilda laments what she calls his "demonic irresistibleness, that magnetic influence felt not only by the other sex but his own". She sees it as an embarrassment, a burden to him, and laments that he could not find it in himself to be unresponsive or unapproachable. Amelia, similarly burdened as Matilda saw it, had managed, it would appear, to keep a cooler head.

Liszt's attractiveness had, in one case at least, disastrous consequences, as Matilda finds when she returns to Weimar ten years later and discovers that Constance is in a hospital for the insane: "Love for Liszt had unhinged her reason!" Matilda exonerates him from blame for the consequences of his fatal charisma. She reserves criticism instead for British hypocrisy. Some English schoolgirls, pupils of his own pupils, were present at Liszt's organ recital in the chapel and he had kindly invited them back to his house. One fourteen-year-old remarked to Matilda as they were making their way there, "Of course, as mamma says, Liszt is a bad man and we ought not to visit him, but attending a concert at his house is quite another matter". "Insular cant!" Matilda exclaims. Those who have moral scruples should stay away. To pass judgement but go all the same for the sake of being able to boast back at home of having heard Liszt play "is just the sort of Philistinism that makes us hated and hate ourselves abroad". Matilda blushed on more than one occasion for the behaviour of her compatriots. "The great drawback of foreign travel is English vulgarity", she wrote in 1900 and once across the Channel she always made a point of avoiding English society whenever she could.

The people she met and the places she went to were the grist to her mill as a novelist and Liszt, under the name Melissus, plays a prominent role in *Felicia*, a novel of 1875, much of which takes place in one of those small German states whose passing into the Greater Germany Matilda much lamented. The fictional re-creation preserves better than the later recollections the impact of his astonishing performances and the quality of personality which bore all before him. With his "slender, sinewy, almost interminable fingers" he performed what seemed miracles: "he now leapt like a skilful chamois hunter from peak to peak, overcoming one by one what had seemed a minute before, superhuman difficulties, finally reaching the highest pinnacle of musical attainment, the point beyond which excellence, mastery, and imaginativeness could not go". His moral code, she concedes, will not bear much examination but: "Whatever else he might be, he stood aloof from insignificance. Even in his trifling you recognised the many-sided, far-visioned, illuminating force of genius. Such a man was a power for good or evil ... there was very little to be done in the way of obstruction".

Felicia is an ambitious novel. *Kitty* made a sweep through society from moneyless and disorderly Paradise Place to the amenities of wealth and a title but *Felicia* lays claim to a different range, an intellectual one this time, which encompasses both theological debate and an understanding of the compulsions of genius. It contains not only the fascinating study of Liszt but also another strong story, that of a man who renounces a promising clerical career because of intellectual doubts. The devout cleric who is driven off course by Darwinism and other blasts of scientific rationalism is a figure first introduced in *Dr Jacob* and developed in several later novels. *Felicia* is a serious attempt to penetrate the personal and moral implications of the choice to be made, whether it is justified to inflict pain on others as well as oneself in pursuit of high-minded purity of motive, and whether the cause of regeneration is not better served by patient fulfilment of duty while quietly working towards general enlightenment, rather than by bold assertions and rejections which may damage more than they can save. It is plain that Matilda is looking for an educated and cultured audience, who can be expected, for example, to read quotations from German and Greek without translation, but the demands of the three-volume novel exact their usual price. The action becomes too diffused as it turns into a rapid tour of prominent European cities and spreads out into ancillary stories which weaken the impact of the strong material centred on Strickland and Melissus. It is to Matilda's credit, however, that she refuses to settle for unrealistic happy endings. Felicia, who marries Melissus in the dazzle of his personality, finds that being married to a charismatic genius is not a bed of roses. Strickland had wanted to marry Felicia himself but renounced her when he forfeited his career prospects by leaving the ministry; he finishes by marrying a woman of inferior birth and is subsequently shamed by her social inadequacies.

The character of Strickland was based on a Dr Thomas Wilson who was among those Matilda encountered in Weimar and who was to be also the prototype of Robert Elsmere, hero of Mrs Humphrey Ward's novel of 1888. Wilson was a friend of George Eliot and George Henry Lewes and also, unfortunately to Matilda's eyes, of Thomas Carlyle, "the apologist of brute force, of blood and iron policy, of slavery", as she calls him. This error apart, she finds Wilson a "most beloved and worthily-beloved man". What particularly attracted her to him was his religious stance which connected intimately with ideas which had been fermenting in her own mind at least since the time when, during the American Civil War, she heard ministers in Suffolk pulpits preaching in defence of slavery. That had put the seal on her alienation from a church which was too much tied to the old conservatism against which she had been a rebel from an early age. Nonconformity as an alternative did not attract her but at no stage of her life could she be content with outright disbelief. It was natural in the circumstances that the history of Dr Wilson should deeply affect her. He was ordained as a young man and likely to rise to prominence but his adherence to the church faltered when he came to look seriously at the Thirty-Nine Articles. Then he saw "clear as day that acceptance of them by any intelligent being must be make-belief, that in consequence his own life was a sham". He gave up his career, moved to Weimar and became a teacher of English in a school for girls but, respected and honourably treated as he was, he was a saddened and frustrated man. He felt he had a message and the gifts to make it heard and his dream was to settle in London and there establish a free church where he could preach a Christianity "untravestied, unadulterated by Councils and Synods, St Augustines and St Athanasiuses". Wilson's struggle to find a home and a form for his strong religious instinct struck a deep chord in Matilda who tried all her life to find some philosophical/religious support for her belief that the proper attitude to life was positive and not, as she complained of Thomas Hardy, negative and pessimistic. "Life is good and wholesome!" she wrote in 1900 at the end of a book of reminiscences, a confidence which underlies her inexhaustible desire to take in as much of what is going on around her as she can. As for the hereafter, she does not speculate.

Also in Weimar Matilda met a young Franciscan monk, an Irishman by birth, who had found in the monastic life of his community an excuse for what Matilda characterises as "sheer self-indulgence". The impact of Darwinism, politics, wars, natural disasters or whatever else might shake the world at large passed over this healthy young man without disturbing his comfort or his conscience one jot. Like Wilson/ Strickland, this young monk becomes the central figure of a novel, *Brother Gabriel*, (1878) but in the novel he is forced out of his spiritual complacency and brought face to face with the human dimensions of love and sacrifice. He loses faith in the creed of denial and suppression he had been brought up to, abandons his calling, involves himself thoroughly in contemporary life, inveighs against the "immorality" of priestly rule, fights for republican France and finally, ill and prematurely old, retires to a country cottage, tends his garden and waits for death. The discarding of what he now sees as pernicious doctrines has cost him the bright hopes of his youth but the novel ends on an up-beat note. Freed from error and lifted "into the light of truth" Gabriel, though dying, is "cured". *Felicia* and *Brother Gabriel* are striking early examples of Matilda's way of making her books out of her life and also of her lifelong rejection of conventional religion and her search elsewhere for life's meaning. Henry James, many years later, remembered his reading of *Brother Gabriel* among other of Matilda's novels.

Felicia had been preceded by *The Sylvestres*, a novel very much centred on current ideas and controversies, in this case the new prescriptions for social and political organisation which were thrown up in the ferment of the French Revolution. *Felicia* extends the ground to take in other areas of contemporary life, a dominant figure in public consciousness in the person of Liszt/Melissus and, with Strickland, the ever-burning question of the future of religion. Many of the novels which follow will be of the same general pattern: an idea or issue of the hour is at the heart of them and a narrative frame, more or less successfully sustained, surrounds it. The desire to stimulate awareness and provoke thought informs almost all of Matilda's work from the 1870s on. It influences her novels and gives them substance though, unfortunately, too often at the expense of subtlety in characterisation and structure, and it takes most obvious form in her commitment to work for the promotion of Anglo-French understanding, a mission which she assumes after a lengthy stay in France in 1874/5.

Matilda's visit to Nantes and its environs in 1874 extended to a twelve months stay with consequences which had a determining influence on the rest of her life. Eugène Bodichon's stories of French domestic and political life had captured her interest in Algeria and attuned her to appreciate what she was now to find. She developed friendships in families whose radicalism reinforced her own political thinking and her experience of Roman Catholicism as an entrenched element in national life intensified her animosity to all institutionalised religion. France confirmed the direction of her own thinking and at the same time enlarged its scope, while for both country and people she developed a deep and abiding love. She became a devoted Francophile and embarked on a long sequence of books, fictional and non-fictional, in which she sought to reduce, if not remove, the misunderstandings, suspicion and outright hostility which historically had poisoned French-English relations. It was a labour of Sisyphus but she stuck to it. What she wrote in this cause has long been superseded, as she knew it would be, but it had a significant role in its day and to read it now is to gain an insight into social history as reported at first-hand by a mentally vigorous observer who was sympathetic but prepared to criticise, severely if need be. It is also to enjoy the advantages of an extensive tour of France, east to west, north to south, seen as it was then through the eyes of a traveller with an ever-alert eye and a gift for description. France with its wider dimensions, the vivacity of its manners and its openness of mind, as contrasted with a more reserved and less supple England — "our gloomy, phlegmatic, insular character" as she describes it in *Brother Gabriel* — made a great appeal to her. Her enthusiastic response to the intellectual challenge presented by France and its history and the stimulus of personal contacts and travel infuse all her writings about France. The life of her indefatigable personality lingers in them still.

Chapter Three

A SECOND NATIVE LAND

Matilda claimed French descent through Huguenot ancestors of the Bethams and family connection and personal sympathy led her to embrace France as a second native land, "my adopted and additional country", she called it. For forty years, even while she kept up her production of stories and novels with other backgrounds, she poured out a stream of articles and books devoted to France, its history, its customs and its topography. She also wrote novels and stories which are either set in France or in which French characters predominate. From 1874 until 1906, when a breakdown warned her that the annual visits were becoming too much, she went every year for visits in which she eventually covered every part of the country, including areas to which the English rarely penetrated. She wrote about what she saw, filling out and substantiating observation by enquiry on the spot and by the study of government publications, scholarly books, classic works and the latest publications. The earliest of the books, *A Year in Western France*, comes directly out of the year-long visit of 1874/75; the last, *Twentieth Century France* (1917), was the fruit of long and passionate identification with the fortunes of her adopted country. She had suffered with the defeated in 1870, felt personal anguish at the forfeiture of Alsace-Lorraine and shared the bitterness of social and political reformers when their hopes and projects were frustrated. Her final word is of satisfaction that out of all the turmoil of the century a better-ordered society is taking shape. Since the establishment of the Third Republic, she writes, "French progress is not opinion but checkable fact".

It was a source of particular gratification to her that the signing of the Entente Cordiale in 1904 held out a hope of better relations between France and England, the aim to which all Matilda's Francophile energies had been directed. Writers, she argued, had a particular contribution to make to this through what, in an article of 1909, she describes as "literary internationalisation ... the fruitful, interesting and hitherto neglected study of nation by nation". Other novelists who might have exerted a beneficent influence had not only failed to contribute to this, she complains, but actually militated against it. Dickens, for example, when he wanted a stage villain produced M. Blandois in *Little Dorrit* or Mlle. Hortense in *Bleak House*. French novelists were no better. The villain of *The Three Musketeers* must, "of course", be an Englishwoman and "Balzac piled up a Pelion on Ossa of

Britannic vices when portraying 'Miladi Dudley". Such casual insults, Matilda argued, reflected widespread prejudice and animosity on both sides and contributed to a situation which was not only regrettable but potentially dangerous. The natural gifts and qualities of the two nations were different but their free institutions, their literature, science, arts and economic conditions put them both in the vanguard of progress and conflict between them "would retard the progress of civilisation for centuries". Always alert to the currents of contemporary life, she undertook to play a part as mediating and conciliating influence.

Differences of temperament between French and English, attractive or repellent according to mood and circumstance, together with a history of national conflict, the most recent episode of which was vividly present within living memory, combined to make Matilda's task a formidable if not impossible one. France, "the old enemy" was firmly fixed in English minds as a source of military, political, intellectual and moral danger. In days when only a small minority travelled abroad and many never left the place where they were born, the image of Napoleon as "old bogey" fed deep-seated distrust and animosity towards the near and, so it seemed, ever-threatening neighbour. Military invasion lurked as a possible threat and the contagion of French revolutionary ideas hung in the atmosphere as a menacing presence, taking specific form from time to time, as in the Chartist riots of 1848 which coincided with a further revolutionary eruption in continental Europe. Among the uneducated and less sophisticated there was even doubt as to whether the French could properly be called human at all. Mrs Brindle, "an angular, uncouth Suffolk peasant woman" in Matilda's novel *Half-Way* (1888), crosses the Channel with her employer and is surprised to discover bit by bit that "French folks are just flesh and blood like ourselves". In a splendidly characteristic speech at an (Anglo-French) wedding-party she runs through a catalogue of English prejudice: " 'Tis true my grandfather, now in Abraham's bosom, lost a leg at Waterloo, and Bonaparte, as I've heard tell, used to eat little children … and your country, they say, is ready to flare up at any moment like a hay-stack on fire, when all rich people's heads will be cut off as before", yet in spite of all that: "though I say such a thing as least expected to do the same, I find people as harmless in France as elsewhere". As a sign of her conversion she cooks a Christmas pudding to the amazement and enthusiastic admiration of a French family party. Even the slightly more sophisticated young farmer, Abel Gooding, in *A Suffolk Courtship* (1900), is taken aback to find when he meets a Frenchman that he looks and behaves very much like himself. Matilda makes shrewd use of humour as an effective weapon against prejudice but she was very serious in her self-appointed task of informing and stimulating a counter-influence to prevailing hostility and helping to prepare a basis on which mutual tolerance, at least, could be founded.

Suspicion and ill-will were not on one side only. English authors, artists, athletes and intellectuals might all be welcome in France, Matilda writes in 1900, "but England itself, how magnificently is she hated!" Ultramondane detestation of a Protestant and democratic country, she believes, is at the root of this together with jealousy of British colonial expansion. Edward VII's support for the 1904 Entente Cordiale and his international-mindedness gave her hope that his accession to the throne would set a new tone and she is optimistic about the auguries. Hitherto, she says,

> Like naughty, ill-bred little boy and girl making faces
> and nasardes at each other across the road, for years
> John Bull and Madame la République seemed bent
> on coming to fisticuffs. By great good luck the road
> [the Channel] was not easy to cross, and now, grown
> older and wiser, the pair at least blow kisses to each
> other and pass on.

She was very much against the construction of a Channel tunnel when that was mooted. Neighbours get on better, she said, if they do not live too close together.

Her work was taken seriously in France and in 1891 the government bestowed on her the title of Officier de l'Instruction Publique de France in recognition of her services to Anglo-French relations. She was the first English person, man or woman, to be so honoured. At the Franco-British Exhibition of 1908 her work was again acknowledged by the award of a medal and in 1917 her book *Twentieth Century France* was prefaced with a signed portrait of the French President, Poincarré. She complained that she had no official recognition in England though, according to *The Times*, she was awarded a Civil List pension and an obituary written by a Hastings neighbour states that in 1906 Edward VII instructed that a letter be sent her to signify his appreciation of her work, also that in 1916 George V "graciously received" an autograph copy of her novel, *Hearts of Alsace*. Matilda herself makes no boast of Edwards VII's letter or George V's acknowledgement. She probably regarded both as inadequate gestures from her fellow-countrymen but she records gratifying individual instances of attention and esteem from other sources. John Murray in person invited her to bring up to date the *Handbook for Travellers in France*, one of the famous series he had initiated in 1836, and John Morley, statesman, writer and editor, published many of her articles for *The Pall Mall Gazette*: "No one had taken more interest in my studies of French life", she reports, and she credits him, along with Frederic Harrison, a notable figure in several spheres, with giving her the encouragement to undertake and pursue her Anglo-French mission. Lord John Russell, as she does not omit to mention, read and quoted from her. Henry James unfortunately (she thought) said almost nothing about her novels but when they met they talked a great deal about France and Matilda learned that he valued her studies of its life and literature. Lord Kitchener, back from the Sudan, if ignorant beforehand, perforce became aware of her and her work at a meeting of the London Society of East Anglians which Matilda attended and at which Kitchener, "the great Suffolker, vanquisher of the Mahdi and hero of Khartoum", was guest of honour. The episode, told at some length, is an amusing example of Matilda's determination to enlarge her range of distinguished acquaintances and at the same time ensure that some of the limelight focused on them should also fall on her.

It was a prestigious occasion. Rider Haggard, born in Norfolk, educated at Ipswich Grammar School, spoke and, as Matilda tells it, "admiring crowds" looked on as "we fortunate ones —that is to say, East Anglians" — dined. The scene, she remarks, was reminiscent of those days when Parisian crowds used to gather to watch their monarch and family eat. She appears to have found the experience gratifying rather than otherwise. The chairman of the gathering was Sir Arthur Spurgeon, head of the publishing house of Cassell and, almost inevitably, it seems, one of Matilda's acquaintances. Others merely shook hands with Kitchener but Matilda asked Spurgeon to allow her the privilege of a few minutes conversation with the great man. This was granted whereupon, speaking in French, she passed on to him the congratulations on his late victory conveyed to her by "my old and valued friend, the late General Nicola, former military governor of Paris." Kitchener replied in French also, speaking the language "as to the manner born and without the faintest English accent" (which is more than she could say of herself, Matilda adds). To have engaged his interest was a feather in her cap which she duly shows off. She is proud of her initiative in approaching him and reports the envy of onlookers. She is also candid enough to report that some among her friends were shocked that she had joined in a celebration of the Sudan campaign and Kitchener's role in it. Rights and wrongs of this imperial episode apart, the story of the dinner is a telling and amusing example of Matilda's determination not to allow her light to be hidden under a bushel — as an ambitious woman with her living to make she had to be a self-publicist — but it is also evidence of the real respect which her name and reputation as a Francophile commanded.

Matilda's career as student of France and promoter of France to the under-informed and unsympathetic English began effectively with the twelve-month stay she made in 1874/5. *A Year in Western France*, the first fruit of this visit, is a foretaste of the themes and character of the books that follow. To call them simply "reports on France" would be an accurate enough description of their contents but would not do justice to their life and character, Matilda's resources as a writer and her vigorous personality. From the early days when ambition first dawned and she determined to make a place for herself in the great world, she had set it down as a first essential that she must cultivate acquaintance as widely as possible, not only among the Spurgeons and Kitcheners of the world but with all sorts and conditions of men and women. Her capacity to make friends and to make herself acceptable across the social spectrum, not only in England but, even more remarkably, in France too, was an invaluable gift and it was also a skill which she cultivated as her prime instrument for gathering material for her writing and impressing it with personal knowledge, personal reaction and the insight born of close experience. She honed her technique in her early forays into the social world of London and she enlarged and refined it in France. *In Twentieth Century France* (1917) she claims that during the forty odd years that she has been travelling in France she has met and talked to representatives of every section of its life, political, military, professional, literary, artistic, commercial and agricultural. Her contacts included officers of the Legion of Honour and members of what she calls "highly cultivated social centres" throughout the length and breadth of France; but as well as the educated and the influential, she valued also the characters of small shopkeepers and peasants from whose experience and conversation she was always willing to learn. In days when comparatively few travelled and those who did confined themselves by and large to well-trodden routes and to cosmopolitan hotels, she stayed whenever possible in private homes and she took pride in being what she called a "devious traveller" who in her inexhaustible pursuit of whatever might be of interest rejoiced in "protracted zigzaggeries — preposterous peregrinations", rejecting tight itineraries and schedules but taking advantage of every opportunity to see whatever or whoever of interest there might be.

She had a notable example in cousin Amelia who in 1873 had published *Untrodden Peaks and Unfrequented Valleys*, the account of a pioneering expedition which she had made in the Dolomites accompanied by a friend, Lucy Renshawe. The two women had rapidly become impatient with their courier who wanted them to keep to prescribed paths and well-appointed hotels, whereas they wanted to venture into new areas and meet the people who lived there. They dismissed the courier and struck out on their own to their great personal gain and the benefit of the book which Amelia wrote on their return. The example was not lost on Matilda. She also would have no time for a conventional tourist itinerary and she also would accept physical effort, discomfort and even a degree of risk (less it must be said than in the Dolomites) and leave nothing undone or unseen that it was possible to do or see.

Amelia's book offered an example of spirited and original travel-writing and no doubt Matilda took note of it in all its aspects but when she embarked on her French books she had at hand also an earlier example and one whose concerns were more immediately relevant to her own. This was Arthur Young (1741-1820), famous agriculturalist, Suffolk man and farmer, whose book, *Travels in France* (1792), became and remained a bible of agricultural wisdom but was famed also for its reporting of French life and society in the period just before the outbreak of revolution and during its early days. Matilda as farmer and writer was proud to say that she walked in Young's footsteps. His influence is widely diffused in her French books and she repaid it by an edition of *The Travels* and also of his autobiography, work which brought her unqualified praise at the time and a lasting reputation as a worthy and unchallenged authority on Young.

Young's agricultural career had begun inauspiciously as a persistent and serially unsuccessful farmer but from early experience he derived the knowledge to look at other farms with a discriminating and expert eye and he embarked on a series of tours of England, studying as he went the state of agriculture in the various regions. These reports were warmly welcomed not only for their picture of farming but also for the general information they contained and he went on to make a similar survey of Ireland. His first French tour in 1787 came about at the invitation of friends to join them on a holiday expedition and this, together with a second visit a year or so later, resulted in his undertaking an extensive exploration of rural France. In 1792 he published an account of his findings and his impressions and the resulting book, *Travels in France*, brought him international fame and influence. His object as he defined it was no less than to ascertain "the Cultivation, Wealth, Resources, and National Prosperity of the Kingdom of France" but for the form of his book he chose to print his diary, "just as it was written on the spot". The consequence is that *Travels in France* is an entertaining as well as meaty book, rich in incident and reflection and full of personal detail, including day-to-day experience of hotels, good and bad, of roads, of sanitation (French "necessary houses" he describes as "temples of abomination") and theatres (he was an avid theatre-goer). He records encounters with seigneurs and peasants and great figures of state and seeks out everything and everyone he can to fill out his picture of a whole community on the verge of world-changing events. He saw the build-up to revolution and its climax with the result that his book becomes a state-of-the-nation report, by a disinterested but keenly alert traveller, on a sensational period of French history. Young's own personality, "lively, charming, spirited", as Fanny Burney described him, makes its impress on everything, whether his spontaneous reactions to people and events or his notes on the farms and farmers he seeks out.

Matilda had every reason to admire his work. She welcomed him as a Suffolk man and, as one who had been intimately acquainted with farm life, even for a time been a farmer herself, she had a considerable measure of fellow-feeling. "The fact is, I am essentially of a practical turn," she remarked once. "The French peasant and his pig ... interest me more than the lately discovered portrait of Joseph's Pharoah" — unlike, of course, cousin Amelia who was certainly interested in Pharaohs and is not known to have had a partiality for pigs. There may have been some sting in Matilda's choice of comparison but there is no doubt that the French peasant and all that was his concerned her greatly, as did every aspect of the French life and society which Young observed and reported. She herself on her own extensive travels up and down the country, in conscious imitation of her "great predecessor" as she calls him, cast a professional eye on the quality of the soil, the kind of crop, the state of the farmhouses — in fact, everything that bore on the life of the land and the people who lived on it. Armed with invaluable cards of introduction, she observed and made knowledgeable enquiries about agricultural methods in every area she visited, culling advice and information from gentlemen farmers and peasant owners and, in the course of her researches, coming to know "the other half of the French population, the half whose interests are bound up in the soil".

Young and Matilda had farming in common but his *Travels* held an additional appeal for her in the light it shed on events at a climactic time in French history. This gave his work an irresistible appeal to her radical spirit though Young's own attitude was moderate. He sympathised with the anguish of the poor and recognised the abuses of the feudal system and the *grands seigneurs* and he denounced the misdeeds of the government; but he was no democrat. Only men of property, he believed (and certainly not women) should have a voice in government. Matilda greatly admired him nonetheless. By 1888 she had herself become a widely experienced traveller in France and she put up a suggestion to the publisher George Bell that she should prepare a new edition of *Travels in France,* complete with an introduction and biographical sketch by herself. Bell agreed and offered her forty pounds for it which she was pleased to accept. As was usual with her, she was more interested in the task than in the money. To edit Young would be "a labour of love", she said, but money was needed nevertheless and shortly afterwards she had to ask for an advance to help her with the cost of visits to Suffolk to meet Arthur Young's grandson and to enable her to buy necessary books. For final payment Bell sent her ten pounds more than originally agreed, certainly not too much for the amount of work she put into it. The introduction in particular is a substantial piece of work in which Matilda draws on the deep and extensive knowledge she has acquired over the years for a comparison between the contemporary situation in France and the way things were when Young was writing. Her edition still holds its ground by virtue of its thoroughness and its scholarship.

Travels appeared at a time when Anglo-French relations were undergoing one of their periods of severe strain but the merits of her work were recognised and appreciated all the same. She was particularly proud that Oxford University included it in the Modern History tripos. Eager to take advantage of the kudos this brought her she undertook and in 1898 published an edition of Young's autobiography and correspondence, another time-consuming and demanding piece of work for which she abridged and arranged seven packets of manuscript material and twelve folio volumes, providing full annotations throughout. Both volumes, the edition of *Travels* and that of the autobiography, reflect in their scrupulous research and scholarly thoroughness another facet of this gifted woman. With similar concentration of talent and effort in more widely known areas she might have won a lasting reputation to equal her cousin's but her interests were too diffuse and her nature too gregarious to allow of it.

Young's influence on Matilda's career as a chronicler of French life and character was a determining one. In his preface to *Travels* he emphasises the difference between himself and other writers on France. There are "very curious enquiries" to be made, he says, about the foundations of the French national economy but "those whose political rêveries are spun by their fire-sides, or caught flying as they are whirled through Europe in post-chaises" are not in a position to answer them. He, by contrast, has travelled widely and slowly and looked and listened on the spot. Matilda takes up the point at the beginning of her introduction to *Travels* and applies it to her own work. Her knowledge of France, is, she says, "after Young's own fashion — the fruit of investigations as lovingly and laboriously pursued as those of my great predecessor". She has followed in his footsteps, literally and metaphorically, and travelled even further into every district of France. Like Young, also, she has studied not only the state of agriculture but the social, political and economic conditions of France as far as the most diligent and thorough enquiry and observation can take her. Young's book paints an invaluable picture of France on the cusp of momentous events and Matilda is unstinting in her admiration as she draws it to the attention of English readers but at the same time she is anxious to make it plain that great changes have taken place in the years since he wrote and great strides forward in all areas of French life. This is the theme of her introduction to *Travels* in which she goes district by district through Young's account, drawing attention to contrasts between then and now. The theme of progress, thus firmly emphasised, is taken up and developed more fully in *France of To-Day*, which Matilda published in 1892 and which Frederic Harrison called "a necessary sequel" to Young's "indispensable book". The sub-title is *A Survey Comparative and Retrospective* and Matilda is at pains to stress the improvements flowing from release of energy and hope with the founding of the Third Republic after 1870. Agriculture like everything else had improved by leaps and bounds since Young's day but Matilda, always fondly attached to memories of Suffolk in her youth, cannot repress a twinge of regret at the all-dominating new farm machinery which in France and elsewhere was rapidly supplanting ancient methods and appliances. It might be efficient but it was not picturesque. *In France of To-Day* she deplores "the complete prosaicisation of rustic life" and looks without enthusiasm to a future when the idyllic element will quite vanish and all will savour, she says, of Chicago!

In her accounts of her observations and responses she does not print straight from a diary as Young did but she retains a diary-like sense of immediacy and she makes use of a diary's liberty to introduce anecdote and eccentric episode as they occur. Her tone like Young's is one of informal communication, the easy, personal voice of a friend recounting the events of the day, the interesting persons met and the noteworthy sights seen. Young reserved his more substantial farming material for separate publication but there are no divisions in Matilda's record as day-to-day events and descriptions lead without break into more or less substantial commentary on whatever topic has been suggested by the occasion. Some subjects recur as major preoccupations but Matilda is very willing to give room to any which she thinks will be informative and enlightening. Thus, in *A Year in Western France* she incorporates a lengthy summary of a recently argued theory concerning the history and function of the great stones at Carnac, which were unknown to Young, and also a long extract from the report of a Commission of Enquiry into the causes of the Commune. This practice of quotation or summary, sometimes lengthy, is one that she maintains throughout her career to give extra range and substance. When necessary she offers her own translation of a relevant passage of poetry or prose. Her focus, like Young's, is on rural and provincial France and she takes a particularly sympathetic interest in the lives of peasants. She enjoyed, for example, the hospitality (cider and rye bread) that she was offered in a Breton farmer's cottage and she noted with appreciation the quality of the furniture which stood on the bare and dirty earth floor: "There was a beautiful old carved wardrobe, with brass clasps, all as bright as gold, and the whole interior was an odd mixture of squalor and solid ease, if not comfort". In her accounts of country people Matilda is honest, non-judgmental and non-patronising and she is often admiring. What she saw of peasant life reinforced very strongly her conviction that ownership of land, however small the holding, made all the difference to the quality of lives and characters. With the confidence of ownership the peasants, she found, were sober, hard-working, at ease in company and possessed a natural dignity but where they had no land or property, as in Normandy, they were in every way inferior and intemperance was the curse of the region. To such as they Zola's picture of rural life and peasantry was fitting but as a general portrait of peasant life Matilda always indignantly repudiates it.

She refers to Zola on a number of occasions but does not attempt a larger *critique*. She was widely read in French literature and made a point of keeping herself and her readers familiar with such contemporary work as might be of interest to them, as in a late book, *Literary Rambles in France* (1907) where she discusses Flaubert, George Sand, de Musset and others. She is notably relaxed about the relations between George Sand and Alfred de Musset. "Both were in some measure enfants du siècle and victims of an epoch", she writes, "and, brave in the face of calumny during her lifetime, George Sand has fearlessly challenged the verdict of posterity". Matilda was not a prude as evidenced by her uncomplicated acceptance of Barbara Bodichon's Leigh Smith background and of the relations between George Eliot and George Henry Lewes. It was the later marriage to John Cross that she disapproved of. But she does not engage with Zola and others of his ilk except for the occasional reference. In a late essay, cousin Amelia refers with distaste to "a depraved school of so-called realistic fiction" across the Channel. Matilda merely says that it is not realistic enough as it leaves out too much, just as Zola in her view distorts the "reality" of French peasant life. The latest movements in end-of-century art and literature are outside her range but she has a deep fund of knowledge and a sensitive appreciation of the artistic and historic connections of the areas through which she travels and draws attention in all her travels to notable buildings, historic memorials and connections with eminent figures in the literary or artistic world.

As befits a countrywoman, her descriptions of the natural world are knowledgeable and appreciative whether of birds, plants or the grander spectacles of mountain and river and she is contemptuous of those among her compatriots, "tourists in search of disappointment" she calls them, who adopt an attitude of supercilious unresponsiveness to even awe-inspiring sights. There is a good deal of pleasure to be had from her descriptions of journeys in, for example, *East of Paris* (1902) or an earlier book, *The Roof of France* (1889), which records particularly adventurous forays into areas barely heard of, much less visited, by the English or even by many French.

She paints nature well but much as she loved the countryside, pastoral retreat was not her style. Young encouraged her to write of farms and farming but, beyond that, his lively and uninhibited response to the society in which he found himself and his free and incisive comments on events as they unfolded gave her a licence to spread her own net as widely as she chose. As a result, the vigour of her commentaries on every aspect of French social and political life as she encountered it adds bite and savour to the travel book aspect of her work. She is rarely, if ever, bland and in so far as she is a travel guide, she is one with attitude, who laces instruction and entertainment with firmly enunciated views. She lived through a dynamic period and made the most of her opportunities to savour it. Memories of the tumultuous and terrible events of 1870 were still alive when she went to Nantes in 1874 and their consequences were all about her. She continued to write till the end of the First World War, a span of time in which history moved at an unprecedented rate. With all its lack of system, with the recycling of already used material and with the propensity in later years to indulge in blatant book-making — putting a number of old and new unconnected pieces between two covers — Matilda's personal record of her loving exploration of France and her treatment with vigour and self-confidence of the dominant issues which events threw up can still amuse, stimulate and inform. Her grand project of internationalisation sustains these books and so does a backbone of the sort of topics — social conditions, political orientation, the place of religion in society — which change their form with the passing of time but retain their essential identity. Arthur Young, agriculturalist, commented freely on political affairs as they came within his view. As for Matilda, her political views seem to have been bred in her bones together with her farm-born addiction to the life of the land. Empires and republics might come and go but she stood firm by the conclusions she had formed long ago and she clung undaunted through all vicissitudes to the pillars of her political faith: republicanism, socialism and anti-clericalism.

Hugo and Gambetta were her heroes and she saw and heard both of them. Victor Hugo in 1878 was an old man who read his speech with difficulty but when he welcomed the English among his audience on behalf of France she had no doubt of his personal right to speak for his country. She heard Gambetta twice. The first time was at Versailles, again in 1878, when he too, though comparatively young, seemed worn down with the burdens of his life, "grey, haggard and a mere wreck", but on the second occasion she rejoiced to recognise the personality which had made him so powerful a figure in "the first really representative government established in France", the Third Republic. The achievements of that government have been great, she believes, but she has no illusion that the earthly paradise has been attained. Endemic problems still cast their shadow, among them Roman Catholicism which remains, as it always is to her, a blight on French society. Priests wield a powerful influence, especially over women, and use it to put a drag on all progressive and reforming effort. Religious schools are pernicious in their conduct and their effect, cramping the permitted range of study and crushing any instinct to intellectual enquiry. As a subsidiary effect the nuns, who produce garments and grow food and take no profit, undercut the poor who need to make their livings by their industry. The pilgrimage to Lourdes, a great religious set-piece, is to her eyes "a heart-breaking exhibition of credulousness and fraud, paganish gullibility and unblushing imposture". The ceremony of taking the veil utterly horrifies her by its violation of human feeling. Her revulsion from conventual life, from French ultramontanism and virtually everything associated with Roman Catholicism is rooted in her whole approach to religion but it acquires a strongly political colouring in France when her natural antipathy takes fire from her radicalism. Her independent adoption of a strong line is highlighted in *The Times* obituary which points out that her views, though common enough in the twentieth century, were developed by her at a date when the reaction fostered under MacMahon's presidency was at its height and the triumph of Catholicism seemed assured.

Alongside religion, education is one of the dominating motifs of Matilda's commentary and *A Year in Western France* devotes two chapters to it. Matilda is impressed by the cultural resources commonly available in provincial towns and contrasts the situation with that in England. Steadfast though she was in refusing to be caught up in Barbara Bodichon's enthusiasm for the higher education of women, she was always glad to note good provision for girls in schools and art colleges and she commends Nantes for offering free musical instruction to adults of both sexes. Ladies there also attended courses in botany and chemistry among other subjects. Education in a broader sense, however, as a preparation for life, she finds seriously wrong-headed and here the comparison with England works very much against France. The great fault in the French notion of the proper bringing-up of the young is, Matilda argues, over-supervision. A properly-brought-up young French lady in bourgeois society as Matilda first knew it was not allowed to walk out alone, much less to enjoy vigorous exercise. From a child, even from babyhood, she was ridiculously over-dressed and so unable to play freely or walk vigorously. On all outings, however small, she had to be accompanied by a servant and unmarried women, even when long past youth, did not venture out without their maid. Their young lives being so restricted it was no wonder, Matilda writes, that marriage was hailed by them as a release into a kind of liberty, even though marriage itself was rarely a matter of love or even compatibility. The *dot*, or dowry, was the all-important consideration: " 'Falling in love', all circumstances considered, must be an almost unheard-of phenomenon in French society".

Boys fared little better for whatever kind of school they went to, clerical or secular, they were under perpetual supervision from morning to night. At school and seminary alike they were treated "precisely as if they were prisoners of the most perverted and dangerous class, ready at any moment to break away and commit some new offence". Deprived of all freedom of speech or action they behaved like automata, unable to develop or express any individuality. Young girls contracted loveless marriages but at least found themselves a rôle as housewives and mothers into which they poured their energies but the boys had no such safety-net. Once released from school they were likely to fall into all kinds of dissipation in reaction to the unnatural restraint into which they had been forced. The humiliation of Sedan, Matilda judges, was largely owing to the upbringing of the officer class: it had failed to nurture in them the strength of character which was needed.

Under the Third Republic things were gradually to change and energies would be released in the field of education as elsewhere. Matilda's 1917 description of schooling in twentieth century France paints a very different picture from the one of earlier years. Now, under the new regime, "Taste, the faculty of observation, the artistic sense, are developed, and character is formed. It could not be otherwise in the case of so highly cultured and so intellectual a nation". A law of 1881 required that all teachers must have a recognised qualification and the opening between 1880-82 of public day-schools for girls throughout France dealt "a first blow" to convent schools — Matilda looks forward hopefully to the eventual disappearance of convents themselves. Encouraged by evidence of the reform which she sees all around her, she is prepared to take a fresh look at other things that she previously found uncongenial or seriously to be deplored, including the dowry. Her initial reaction had been to dismiss it as a thoroughly bad thing but later, with a strengthened belief in the fundamental soundness of French social life, she defends it as an element in a coherent and carefully judged system governing family units. Guarded zealously as the bedrock of society, the close-knit French family provides support for its members but it also imposes restraints. The French, Matilda explains, are not given to free-handed generosity but husband family funds with care, having in mind always the needs of later generations. Consequently, with an eye to the future they confine themselves to one or two children, unlike the English who improvidently breed large families. With similar care for family resources, the financial circumstances of bride and groom are the overriding consideration in any projected marriage, for financial or other failure on the part of any member of the family circle redounds on every other member of it. Far from being flighty, as the English stereotype has it, the French, Matilda argues, are serious, unsentimental and logical in the ordering of their lives, what they lose in romance being compensated by other gains: "For myself I have found wedded life in France uniformly peaceful and happy". She contrasts this with "our own English voluntaryism", by which she means the freedom of young English men and women to choose their own partners without submission to prudent parental guidance. The result is that modern liberty "run mad, is responsible for the unhappy and wretched marriages so common here in all ranks".

Matilda responds to what she sees in the context of the time when she sees it. Her views develop and change as over the years she sees French society develop and change. In spite of disasters and disappointments, nothing can shake her first impression that France is without parallel among European nations. Its family life may be unromantic, its political life turbulent, its treatment of animals cruel (a subject on which she feels strongly), but no other country possesses "that gay, gracious, and indescribable, abundantly-gifted character which renders the French people the most brilliant, fascinating, and delightful in the world". As for French women, though relegated in the Napoleonic code to the perpetual condition of minors and idiots, they nevertheless reign supreme in the home with all the power that a family-centred society gives them. In a mood of enthusiasm Matilda sweeps away all reservations, together with orthodox sentence structure: "Frenchwomen are without doubt the cleverest, the most gifted beings in creation — though she may be ignorant of a thousand facts humdrum folks are bound to know". In *Twentieth Century France*, Matilda finds them also the best dressed in the world with the famous "indefinable something that is wholly native and not easy of imitation". Over-attention to dress had been one of her severest criticisms of French life as she earlier encountered it but the temper of society is now changed and she is happy to add elegance of costume to the other excellencies which she finds in French life.

Unfortunately, French elegance highlights English deficiencies. Earlier Matilda had remarked with disapproval that French women took no exercise but when later they find their feet, literally and metaphorically, it seems that they turn walking into an art: "Without hurry or flurry, with head erect and skirts gracefully caught up, they are every whit as graceful out of doors as they are in the drawing room". Regrettably, she adds, the same cannot be said of twentieth century English girls. She is pleased that they now spend a great deal of time out of doors, to the benefit of their health, but:

> Pleasant as is the picture of a girl golfer, cheering as is the contemplation of glowing health and robustness, one turns away with a sigh. Swinging her arms as she goes, taking long strides, wearing a frock up to her knees, the most unbecoming head-gear imaginable, she quickly disenchants the beholder.

This, so redolent of late nineteenth century debates and disapproval of "the girl of to-day", shows Matilda ambiguous as ever about the future role of women. Like other women of her generation she had difficulty in defining precisely what she wanted from female emancipation. Conceding nothing of confidence in women's abilities and their right to develop them to their fullest, she yet clung with one part of her mind to an image of grace and dignity and a specifically female kind of distinction. She could never quite shake off her sense that women could become too emancipated. She draws attention to the war work done by them, she inveighs again French sex-discrimination laws and applauds measures to dilute them but she yet sees clear limits to the extent to which women could or should throw off the traditional sexual characteristics. She writes with approval of a French novel in which the heroine, a successful barrister, is obliged to give up her profession when she has a child: "Nature had re-affirmed her irrevocable law. Socially the world may be turned upside down a thousand times. Motherhood remains". In other words sex imposes non-negotiable conditions and social theory fails against them. Matilda was an adventurous and in many respects bold woman but she was never prepared to go the whole way with feminism and for her own part she kept clear, deliberately or not, of the acid test of marriage.

Home Life in France (1905) brings together in thirty-five summary chapters the findings of her forty years experience of French homes and French families and it is a fascinating work of social history, full of detail and full of substance. It is descriptive and explicatory, covering subjects as divers as the idolisation of the baby in French households, the role of the Juge de Paix and the life of a conscript doing his obligatory national service. The tone is of friendly discourse directed to reasonable people who genuinely want to learn about their neighbours. In a chapter on characteristics she discusses national traits and idiosyncrasies and sums up her experience of French character: "If I were asked ... to focus in a sentence my experience of French character, I should say that, intellectually and socially, here [in France] civilization has reached its highest expression". High civilisation may not be compatible with good business sense, however, and in *Anglo-French Reminiscences* of 1898 Matilda tells the story of a Frenchman whom her brothers knew in Ipswich and who often visited the family home: "He was a very typical Frenchman", she writes, "and an observation he dropped at this time has ever seemed to me a key to French character". The observation, as she reports it, was: 'I take great care not to increase my business'. "Have we not here an explanation of the social and economic problems that well-nigh drive French statesmen to desperation?" Matilda writes and adds "...when men take great care not to increase their business, no statesmanship can do the work for them". She would have found too near the knuckle to be amusing President George W. Bush's alleged remark that the trouble with the French is that they have no word for entrepreneur.

In addition to the non-fiction are Matilda's novels set in France in which French men and women naturally play principal roles. Exceptionally, *The Sylvestres* of 1871 is set in England but it nevertheless has to be counted as the first of the French novels since it is strongly infused with French ideas and resonates with the repercussions of contemporary French history. The last of the group, *A Close Ring* of 1907, makes a close analysis of the social fabric of France itself and embodies Matilda's most mature thinking about French family life and her attempts over the years to balance its pluses and minuses. Three others come between, *Half-Way* (1889), *A Romance of a French Parsonage* (1892), and *A Romance of Dijon* (1894). All of them contain fascinating material and, if they are unlikely to attract a modern readership on their novelistic merits alone, they are certainly worth attention in the context of the Victorian literary and social scene. In an article of January 1894, *The Times*, describing Matilda as "a popular novelist of long standing", remarks justly of her France-inspired novels that "such are her understanding of the people and her gift of picturesque description that her tales seldom fail to yield interest and recreation". The pictures of French domestic life in these books animate the accounts given in the non-fiction and their main plots dramatise the two central elements of all Matilda's thinking about the body politic in France: the pressure for new social and political structures and the contrary force exerted by the baleful and all-embracing influence of Roman Catholicism. The leavening power of humour, invariably present to some degree in all Matilda's writing, is a welcome counter-balance to the serious points and purpose which lie at the heart of all the novels.

Publication of *The Sylvestres* followed Matilda's Christmas in Ryde with Barbara Bodichon, George Eliot and George Henry Lewes, at a time when France and its troubles were much in everyone's mind. As George Eliot had written in *Felix Holt* of another time of political upheaval, so in 1870 "the electrical condition of the clouds in the political hemisphere" forecast "unusual perturbations" and France's struggles to give body to the ideals of the Revolution were only one manifestation of a wider movement extending beyond France. The Ryde party was much interested in Matilda's account of the 1864 Marxist meeting and on this or some other occasion during that week she seems to have been encouraged to tell them about her latest novel in which the clash of old systems and assumptions against the force of new and revolutionary ideas is given the unexpected setting of a quiet English village. In *The Sylvestres* a dramatic and eventually violent series of events is initiated when a centuries-old way of life is disrupted by the sudden appearance of a group of political activists from the Continent who settle into the deeply conservative community. Lewes at least was interested in what he heard and gave Matilda an introduction to Tauchnitz on the strength of it. The reactions of the reading public when the book was published split in predictable ways. It first appeared as a serial in *Good Words* whereupon many readers of this family magazine withdrew their subscriptions, shocked to the core by the open enunciation of ideas quite outside the pale of their thinking. On the other hand and equally foreseeably, working men and women, intellectuals and free-thinkers in general who were united in opposition to the present power structure, were delighted with the book. The novel is a period-piece today but hardly outdated.

The story is of a young woman, Ingaretha, twenty-six years old but still "a happy child". [The name is a legacy from a medieval Betham ancestress. In addition to her pride in the Bethams, Matilda has a regrettable penchant at this period for increasingly preposterous names. She also has an abiding habit of describing young, though fully adult, women as though they were scarcely out of the nursery. She herself was thirty-five in 1871 but still thought of herself and her potential as at no more than an early stage.] Ingaretha has returned from five years travel abroad to take up her responsibilities as mistress of the manor in an idyllic Suffolk village which also has a remarkable name: St Beowulf's Bury. She has the sincerest intentions to do good with the influence her position and her money will give her but, as the novel opens, the question of how to translate intentions into action is troubling her. In spite of her immaturity she shows some signs of independence of mind and character. She finds the society of her eminently respectable, middle-class neighbours dull and she disappoints the expectations of the whole village by refusing the hand of Carew, a somewhat older man who is like herself a local landowner, and who has long been in love with her. Socially and intellectually he is thought by everyone to be the ideal match for her. In the course of the novel she will engage herself to a man of an entirely different background and character whom everyone considers totally unsuitable but, as every novel reader will rapidly forecast, she does finally accept Mr Carew. So far, so predictable and so uninteresting but inside this somewhat soggy envelope there turns out to be much harder, tougher material and the novel springs a surprise in its early pages.

Ingaretha and a few of her dull and worthy neighbours, including the rector, are at tea in her lovely, rose-filled garden when there suddenly appears a totally incongruous sight, a man and woman, shabbily dressed and tramp-like, walking slowly and wearily towards them. After a moment's astonishment Ingaretha and Carew both rise to greet the pair warmly and enthusiastically, for these are the Sylvestres, well-known to them both from earlier foreign travel. Their entry into the quietly tedious and protected environment of the Suffolk garden signals the intrusion of a diametrically different world. M. Sylvestre is of English birth but has Frenchified his name in honour of his French wife and is, to all intents and purposes, a cosmopolitan. They are dedicated Fourierists and Ingaretha had once lived for a week with the two of them in an Algerian phalanstery. The phalanstery had collapsed, defeated by human nature and also by the unremitting hostility of the natural world expressed in an unsupportable climate and the coming of plague among other ills. The deserted phalanstery which she had visited with Barbara Bodichon during their African excursion is obviously in Matilda's mind. Fourier's idealism had failed its practical test there but as late as *In French Africa* Matilda refused to believe that it had been entirely without fruit. In *The Sylvestres*, written within a few years of the visit and with ideas and impressions still fresh in mind, she sets out to weigh up what she sees as the good and hopeful elements against what she diagnoses as the unrealistic and therefore useless, even damaging. M. Sylvestre, Fourier's prophet, is an heroic and almost totally admirable figure but, like Fourierism itself, he has a fatal flaw.

Sylvestre and his wife, Euphrosyne (!), are destitute when they arrive at St Beowulf's Bury. At Ingaretha's invitation and by courtesy of her financial support they settle in the village and promptly begin to spread their version of the good life to the villagers. M. Sylvestre preaches secular sermons in which, undeterred by experience, he looks forward to a Fourierist millennium when equality, universal well-being and fraternal love will create the ideal society. His creed turns the conventionally accepted idea of virtue on its head for he believes "in self-development rather than in self-denial, in self-government rather than in self-negation, in fulfilment rather than in repression, in plenary acceptance rather than in desperate abstinence." Crime and misery are not immutable facts of human destiny, he proclaims, but all these evils will vanish as soon as societies rid themselves of inequalities and the poor and oppressed cast off the false doctrines which keep them under. Then the goodness and love which are in all natures will rise to full development and be subject to no distortion. No whit discouraged by previous experience, he loses no time in setting up a miniature phalanstery in St Beowulf's. His sincerity and his gifts and the appeal of his message are undoubted and, if some personal vanity and fondness for adulation are to be detected in him, they may be overlooked as no more than minor weakness; but he is subject to a far more serious defect. Full of compassion for suffering humanity, fired with a vision of how the world should be, exalted by his role in what he sees as a great crusade he is, sadly and fatally, unable to see beyond himself so far as to notice the realities of the other lives surrounding him. He plans to open a centre for art and science for the villagers but has typically failed to notice that most of them cannot read. "Ah!" he says when this is pointed out to him: "That difficulty did not occur to me". He also fails to notice that the villagers, far from being grateful for the benefits he offers them, are in fact suspicious from the first of these foreigners in their midst and that, as time goes on and he pushes them more and more eagerly towards an enlightenment for which they are not ready, they are becoming increasingly hostile.

Sylvestre's unrealistic idealism combined with the villagers' stubborn reluctance to have good done to them produces a tragic result when Sylvestre himself and a young French disciple, who has come hot from involvement in radical circles on the Continent, are killed by a mob in an outburst of violence. Other causes also contribute to the final disaster. There are powerful forces ranged against the Sylvestres in the shape of the rector, representing the church, and Mr Minifie, Ingaretha's land agent, representing commercial interest. Mr Minifie, whose god is money, resents Ingaretha's generosity to the Sylvestres and will drive them out if he can. Mr Whitelock, the rector, is a good man but he worships the established order of things and is distressed beyond measure that what he thinks of as seditious and irreligious doctrine is being preached in his parish. To him all is for the best in the best possible of worlds and he can have no iota of sympathy with those who want to change what he calls "the laws of social custom and the prejudices of right-minded conservatism". Minifie acts out of malice, Whitelock out of a bewildered sense of what is right. Between them they foster an ugly mood in the village which in the end leads to murder as the mob gives vent to festering resentment at do-goodery and also to their sense of outrage at Sylvestre's gospel of social equality, a doctrine so much at odds with that inculcated by church and state and in which they have been steeped since babyhood. Thus ends a Fourierist experiment in a Suffolk village.

The Sylvestres is essentially a social problem novel, born of an acute sense of the injustices and inequalities of society. As such it belongs with many others of the period, among them some of the most famous books by the greatest writers, but Matilda, coming late into the field, approaches it from a fresh angle. The problems of poverty — lack of education, lack of secure livelihood, lack of respect — are put here in an international frame rather than an exclusively domestic one. The members of the Sylvestre group which gathers in St Beowulf's are of several nationalities. They have lived and spread their message in Europe, Africa and America, everywhere resisting the accepted order and urging the creation of a better one. The location is English but the points of reference are primarily French through the experience of René, the young man who dies with M. Sylvestre. The application to England is unmistakeable. England may be free and beautiful but the worm of social injustice is gnawing at its heart, as René puts it, and more will be needed to expel it than private charity such as Ingaretha dispenses. Ingaretha herself is caught in a transition period between the aristocratic principle and Continental radicalism and she wavers uncertainly between fulfilling the traditional Lady Bountiful role in her village and allying herself with those whose hope and aim is to overthrow the old order. With her marriage to Carew she finally dissociates herself from Sylvestre the visionary, and René the clear-eyed and saddened idealist, to whom she was for a time engaged to be married. She takes up her inherited role in the village, accepting the parameters of conventional life but quietly and gently working to bring about improvements. After her venture onto the wilder shores of revolutionary radicalism her return to the harbours of conservatism comes as an anticlimax but, that granted, the book remains a daring challenge to contemporary society particularly considering the date of its publication. The rise and fall of the commune in Paris and the whole saga of dire and bloody events in 1870 France are the dark and dramatic background to Matilda's attempts to introduce her readers to the ethos of revolution. She hopes for sympathy for her exiles who preach the overthrow of all accepted norms of behaviour and government but, while she celebrates their heroic idealism and sacrifice, she in the end rejects their programme of action as unsuitable to the history and traditions of England. The prescription offered at the end of The Sylvestres is in effect, what Sidney Webb was to call "gradualism", a process of progressive adjustment leading inevitably in time to the reforms desired, but she is anxious that the impulse to drive the reform be not lacking.

What she calls "theological thraldom" has its place among social evils in *The Sylvestres*, as for Matilda it always has. The crippling, repressive effects of Roman Catholicism in France are excoriated in the non-fiction books and in *The Sylvestres* the Church of England fares no better. Mr Whitelock, the rector, is not an ill-meaning man but he is intellectually benighted and the doctrine he preaches is utterly indifferent to the needs and feelings of the poor and the disadvantaged. He is equally blind to the claims of women for personal and social fulfilment, sharing, of course, the Church's traditional teaching about their inferiority. Here, as always in Matilda's work, the subject of the nature and role of women is never far out of sight. Gradualism, she believed, would operate to assure the victory of the women's cause even as it would to bring about reform in society as a whole but this faith, far from being an excuse for relaxation, gave her all the greater motive for using her pen to quicken as much as she could the pace at which the "inevitable" arrived. Irony is one of her most effective weapons. Mr Sylvestre, for example, is an enthusiastic believer in the equality of all men but equality of the sexes is an idea which has passed him by. He patronises his wife and can do no better for the future of women than that implied in his rhetorical question to René: "Is it not acknowledged to be the mission of women to enlighten by their instincts, inspire by their beauty, soften by their grace?" This bland disregard of what may be the qualities and aspirations of women in their own right is among the many oblique shots fired in the novel at unequal treatment and prejudicial expectations. A comic variation on the theme occurs when the amiable Mr Stapleton, a village worthy, returns with his wife from a visit to Ingaretha's house and reflects on the enormity of the fact that he has been required by his hostess to meet "a host of tag-rag and bob-tail political exiles". That Ingaretha should have become entangled with such people, he tells his wife, is a direct consequence of her father's rash action in taking his pregnant wife to hear the corn-law debates in Parliament. Mr Stapleton claims that he foresaw and warned the father of the damaging effect on the unborn child of thus exposing the mother-to-be to the world of politics which was so unsuitable to feminine sensibility. "I told him what would happen", he says, and Mrs Stapleton responds placidly: "I thank God I was never brought up to have opinions".

Episodes of sex discrimination have a proper place in a novel about individual freedom but plot complications are introduced at later stages which scarcely cohere and have no real function except to fill out the required three volumes. This is a recurrent weakness in post-*Kitty* novels as Matilda seizes on issues of the moment. They give her books some vibrancy but she is unable to deepen and shape these narratives with the degree of finesse she achieved in *Kitty* where she was entirely in control of her material. Nevertheless Matilda is a skilful craftswoman. The message dominates both character and plot but there is enough of both to hold the interest and as always her descriptions of the natural setting have the charm of intimate knowledge and appreciation. Her comic sense helps her to a nice turn of phrase as in her description of "three rather lone ladies doing gentility on a hundred and fifty pounds a year" or of the Miss Stapletons dressed up for a dinner "like puffy poppies, striped red and white". She has a wide linguistic range and keeps her vocabulary like her ideas up-to-date, as when she refers in passing to homoeopathy and twice uses the phrase "elective affinity". Her sense of social injustice expresses itself in terms of rival political theories rather than, as in Mrs Gaskell's novels for instance, in terms of individual lives whose conditions and sufferings Mrs Gaskell has personally observed, but the book has vitality and some dramatic urgency. It had enough charge, at any rate, to scare off the faint-hearted.

The Sylvestres is full of vitality but it was followed by a period of ill-health serious enough to cause concern and to stem for a time the flow of Matilda's publications. 1872 was a blank year. 1873 produced *Holiday Letters from Athens, Cairo and Weimar* and 1874 a volume of short stories This was a relatively thin crop but in 1875, after her year in France, Matilda was sufficiently recovered to write a full-scale novel, *Felicia*. The opening pages of the next, *Bridget* (1877), suggest an intention to pick up again the themes and Continental background of *The Sylvestres* as once more a peaceful domestic scene is shattered by the unexpected arrival of refugees from France. This time, however, the interlopers are children, economic rather than political refugees. Their father is dead and other relatives being unable to provide for them they come to throw themselves on the mercy of their uncle and aunt in England. The emphasis is on sympathy and generosity: "Aux plus desherités, le plus d'amour" as the epigraph has it but after this opening the story loses all momentum. France and the French background fade quite out of sight and Matilda turns her attention instead to the humiliations inflicted on a proud English working-man by inflexible class prejudice at home. He is offered patronage which will enable him to rise to a higher rung of the social ladder but rejects it as a betrayal of his fellow-workers. In the end he emigrates, not to America, the usual destination, but to India where he has been appointed to lead a team of draughtsmen and designers on a government project to copy works of Indian art. Queen Victoria had assumed her imperial title in 1876 and Freeland's destination is a striking instance of Matilda's keen eye for the topical.

France as a major subject of fiction does not reappear until *Half-Way* of 1886 by which time Matilda's first-hand knowledge has been greatly expanded and deepened. *A Romance of a French Parsonage* followed in 1892. Both novels have at their core Matilda's loathing of all institutional religion and Roman Catholicism in particular but the sub-title of *Half-Way*, "An Anglo-French Romance", holds out promise that the mood in this instance will be optimistic, celebrating friendship and mutual appreciation between the two countries close to Matilda's heart. The book is also a celebration of youth and hope but before these can triumph the destructive negativity of French Roman Catholicism has to be met and defeated. Priestly influence is exposed as particularly pernicious in its effects on the young and vulnerable who are put under pressure to sacrifice their natural vitality and hopefulness on the altar of an oppressive and life-denying creed. The power of the Church and its essentially corrupt nature are strongly emphasised and against them Matilda sets the positives of youthful vitality and healthy enjoyment of the pleasures of life. The lesson to be drawn is foreshadowed at the very beginning by a cheerfully ironic paean to the pleasures of food which culminates in the conclusion that it is cooks rather than martyrs who should be canonized and it is the cookery book not the catechism which should have pride of place on the bookshelf of every household throughout the world. This is Matilda in her most relaxed mood and leads appropriately to the introduction of the young heroine Cameron Joye (a name mercifully reduced to Camma) who has just arrived on her first visit to France. She hales from Ipswich, Matilda's own territory, and her first encounters with France and the French clearly recall Matilda's own early experience and her delight in discovering how congenial the French countryside and the French temperament were to her: "Ineffable first days in France!" she writes, "whose pen can portray them? what careless memory let them go?" The countryside is lovingly evoked and so is Camma's appreciation of the light, gay national temperament which comes to her, as it did to Matilda, as a refreshing change from the heavier, less buoyant English character with its weight of "northern gloom". There is an unmistakeable autobiographical air about all this as Matilda shares with Camma her own excitement at the opening of a new, unexplored and delightful world and rejoices especially in Burgundy, a region where Matilda had close friends and for which she had a particular love.

Camma is, of course, glowingly beautiful and scintillatingly pure and innocent, "a veritable apparition of grace and witchery", but fortunately she is also a lively young woman. Her reason for being in France, however, goes against the whole bent of her temperament: she is on her way to Alsace to serve in a Protestant sisterhood, the Anglican equivalent of a Catholic convent. This is not the outcome of strong religious feeling but simply of the need she feels to do something useful with her life, an urge which others among Matilda's heroines also feel. They may have money, social status and security but they long for something more substantial than the embroidery and sewing which passes for the "work" of middle-class women — what Matilda with her quasi- or qualified feminism contemptuously calls "sham feminine industries". Camma had been expecting to marry her childhood sweetheart, (who also comes from Ipswich), a young man named Millison Methold (Matilda's fancy for preposterous names infects hero as well as heroine in this book) but the engagement has been broken off, a cause of some sorrow on both sides but not of heartbreak. Now, with marriage no longer imminent, Camma needs some other outlet for her youthful energy. To dedicate herself to self-sacrifice in the service of others suggests itself as a possibility and she enthusiastically embraces it.

The reason for the breaking of the engagement is that Millison has unexpectedly determined to enter the Roman priesthood. Profound religious conviction does not propel him any more than it propels Camma but in the throes of a moral crisis he has been seduced into Romanism by wily clerics who seize avidly on the prospect of securing a young and wealthy catch to enrich their prestige and their coffers. When the novel opens he is on his way to Rome to take the vows which will commit him irrevocably but he has hurt himself by a fall from his horse and also become ill with threatened "brain fever", that mysterious illness and ubiquitous standby of the Victorian novel. He and Camma have arrived unwittingly at the same hotel and each of them, in the respective bedrooms and unknown to each other, takes the fancy to dress up in the robes of what they imagine will be their future calling. Sombre and depersonalising as these are, the young people parade excitedly before their mirrors like children playing at dressing up. The scenes are absurd as Matilda meant them to be but there is potential tragedy looming behind them. Misled by false philosophies of self-suppression and renunciation these young people are on the point of throwing away or utterly perverting their lives. In the event they are saved and will learn that the good life is one of affirmation not negation. Human love, in particular, is not to be renounced. Millison has some guilt to expiate and so comes to this lesson by a harder path than Camma who is quite readily deflected from the sisterhood when a French family, brother, sister and grandmother, friends of her dead mother, invite her to spend a few days at their home. The brother, Eugène, (named, no doubt, in compliment to Dr Bodichon) falls in love with her and she, after due maidenly ignorance of either his or her own feelings, agrees to marry him. Millison also is introduced to the French family and falls in love with the sister Jeanne, a widow of twenty-five, three years older than he, but he has entangled himself too deeply with the Roman church to be able to extricate himself easily. The marriages which eventually take place and the salutary, vivifying effects of contact with the French family are designed to illustrate, according to Matilda's own personal creed, the benefits which the soberer English can derive from French esprit. She takes care to point out that this lightness of spirit is not to be taken for frivolity. Eugène, easy-mannered and charming as he is, intends to engage himself seriously in politics (republican, of course) and help to construct a better society. As for Jeanne, his sister, she develops a major role when, on Millison's behalf, she fends off the strenuous efforts of the Roman priesthood to bind the by-then-unwilling Millison to his original commitment.

Since the setting is France, Roman Catholicism is the principal object of attack in this struggle between human values and a life-denying repressive religion but Anglicanism is not left unscathed. Camma's decision to embrace life and Eugène is taken without any of the agony of indecision which afflicts Millison but this does not mean that there is no effort to exert pressure on her to choose otherwise. She has another suitor, Aubrey, a young curate from her native Suffolk who also happens to be travelling on the Continent and he takes the opportunity to renew his proposal of marriage. In spite of his appeals to the conventions and affiliations of the country they both come from, Camma finds no difficulty in rejecting his offer of a life of dutiful domesticity enlivened by rounds of parish duties and she laughs off his narrow-minded suspicions and disdain for everything French. His is an Anglican version of the view of life represented by convents and monasteries and as such motivated by the same unwholesome idea that denial and repression are in themselves admirable. As invariably happens in a Matilda novel, the nature and rôle of women is a topic which arises. Aubrey prides himself on being abreast of the latest social, political and artistic theories but at one new idea he stumbles:

> He could not admit the revolutionary doctrine concerning women. He clung to the old, fond, foolish ideal of a weaker creature, a soft thing, who screams at a mouse, a feminine paragon, who leaves the world to its business and sits in her drawing-room, mending her husband's socks.

Anglicanism and Catholicism alike give priority to the male and Matilda shows her scorn of both when Jeannie takes charge, as she says, of Millison's soul and with irresistible authority fulfils the role of spiritual leader while Millison cowers in the background. This not only inverts the conventional roles in which the man is the experienced partner

Amelia Edwards in maturity.

Matilda Betham-Edwards in maturity.
From The Lady's Pictorial, c1891

whose support and advice strengthen and instruct the pliant female but it is also a dramatic and indeed revolutionary inversion of the roles assigned by church and state.

As for national prejudices, Camma and her French friends acknowledge them but they are dissolved in laughter and mutual appreciation, a process much helped by Mrs Brindle, Camma's faithful nurse. Mrs Brindle brings her native Suffolk idiom and anti-French prejudices with her but as a fount of good sense and pungent sayings she animates the book whenever she appears. Finally she crowns her conversion to (modified) francophilia by making for her hosts a stupendous Christmas pudding which evokes first disbelieving astonishment and ultimately effusive admiration from the French. There is altogether much affectionate reminiscence of Suffolk in this book — it is the home county of Camma and Millison and scenes of his childhood in the meadows besides the Orwell and the Stour come poignantly to Millison's mind when he faces the cost of renouncing the world for the priesthood: "how calm and peaceful and beauteous these memories of the corn country!" Matilda in reminiscent mood brings her native soil and her second, adopted, homeland together in what is on the whole a happy book in which life triumphs over sterility and doom, regardless of national boundaries, and old phobias and outworn shibboleths are discarded as irrelevant.

It may be that some more intimate personal memory is embodied in *Half-Way*. In *Twentieth Century France*, one of Matilda's latest books, she writes in support of her claim to intimate knowledge of France and its people that: "In more than one household, I had a second home to which I could invite myself whenever I pleased". The passage goes on: "I was indeed regarded in one as a future member of the family". The family home referred to here was in Burgundy, where much of *Half-Way* is set. A footnote offers a brief and tantalising expansion of the reference to a possible marriage with a member of the family: "A domestic Anglo-French Entente", it reads, "frustrated by untoward circumstances". Millison Methold, English, immature and weak in character, hardly seems a suitable candidate for the role of lost French lover but that there are echoes of a frustrated attachment in *Half-Way* is plausible nonetheless. A love affair aborted by the man's submission to a sense of religious obligation is the theme of a poem by Matilda, entitled "Irrevocable! A Woman to her Lover" and there is a similar situation in one of the stories in the volume, *Exchange No Robbery* (1883), where a priest who has been forced reluctantly into the church by his father falls in love with an English girl. She first tries to persuade him to turn Protestant but when that fails returns him to his "duty" and his celibate life. The situation is the occasion of a fierce attack on "the iniquity" of enforced celibacy: "it is mortal blindness, not divine ordinance that turns so many priests into vile men".

This short story, or novelette, precedes *Half-Way* by three years, the ideas which are in embryo there being worked out fully in the novel. The fictional treatments and the situation dramatised in the poem may derive from some personal experience, or they may arise from an incident of which Matilda had heard or, equally, they may simply be her working out of such a story as might well arise in the interrelation of the priest and his flock. Whatever its source, it seized her imagination as an example of the ruthless grip of the Roman Catholic church once it was enabled to take a hold. The details of the story may or may not have been close to Matilda's own personal experience but it seems beyond doubt that a romantic attachment once existed between Matilda and a Frenchman. If he is the anonymous "ami français" to whom *Home Life in France* is dedicated in 1905, the relationship survived, in memory at least, for a long time. The blighting of the marriage prospect may have caused her pain but it did not alienate her from France and neither does it dampen the good spirits of *Half-Way*.

That religion — any religion — unless worn very lightly is the enemy of a healthy society and a wholesome individual life is one of Matilda's firmest beliefs and it is the message of *Half-Way*. *A Romance of a French Parsonage*, which follows six years later, makes the same points but there is much less this time of the light and airy spirit which Matilda so much admired in French life and which she celebrated in *Half-Way*. The attack on Roman Catholicism and on all credal religion is if anything even more far-reaching and sustained than in the earlier book. The motivating situation is that of a priest who loses his faith, a story to which Matilda returns several times. It stems initially, like the story of *Felicia*, from her acquaintance in Weimar with Dr Wilson, a man in whom she evidently saw the archetype of an age when men of faith were struggling to reconcile traditional teaching with what science was telling them. Their problems are touched on in the early novel, *Dr Jacob*, and more fully developed in *Felicia* when Strickland, the Anglican priest, finds himself no longer able to subscribe to the Thirty-Nine Articles, and embarks on a journey in reverse of Newman's *Apologia*, one which takes him away from creed and tradition into uncharted post-Darwinian waters. The central figure of *A Romance of a French Parsonage*, Evelard, is a French Catholic version of Strickland in that like him he is intellectually brilliant, socially accomplished and confidently expected to climb to the highest rank; but his doubts about his vocation come initially from different causes. He finds that his instincts as a man run counter to the rules which prescribe the limitations of priestly life and this marks the beginning of increasing doubt as to whether religious teaching had any meaningful relation to the real experience of men and women. His first step is to renounce his Catholic priesthood and become a Protestant pastor. He leaves Paris and becomes minister of a small, remote fishing-cum-farming village in south-west France. One night, as he re-enters his lonely parsonage he senses the presence of an intruder who is found to be, not some ruffian intent on robbery, but, more surprisingly, a young nun from an enclosed order who has taken advantage of a violent storm to escape from the convent, one wall of which abuts Evelard's garden. Like him, she has found life under the Roman discipline intolerable, her yearning for spiritual peace and illumination unsatisfied. He shelters her and eventually recognises her as the love of his life who had been the immediate cause of his leaving the Church. He and Bernarde had fallen in love when he was her confessor, a situation which puts them both, as they believe, in a condition of direst sin. She had sought to make atonement by taking the veil. He had left the priesthood and in time gone further in alienation as he began to question not just himself and his needs and motivations but the creed he had been brought up in. His Christian faith is at that stage unshaken but he preaches and practises it now from within the fold of the reformed church. *A Romance of a French Parsonage*, with its story of damaged lives, struggle between religious commitment and disenchantment and the eventual rebuilding of life on other terms, reproduces in essentials the story of *Half-Way* and returns once again to the evil, as Matilda sees it, of enforced celibacy. The mood this time is more sombre and the situations are driven further — though Evelard and Bernarde are reunited, the traumatic experiences of the convent have taken too much out of her and she fades away and dies.

The ideas which motivate these novels are not new to Matilda but when they were published they had a topical relevance which drew her to write them. The topicality is pointed out in *Half-Way* by Anatole, the servant who stands in the same relation to Millison as Mrs Brindle does to Camma and who shares, in his own Gallic style, her gift of shrewd and pungent commentary on the goings-on of their superiors. It does not take him long to conclude that "This well-favoured, evidently high-spirited and rich young man was one of the recent converts to Rome talked of in the papers". Such migrations from Canterbury to Rome had been periodic in the nineteenth century ever since the Oxford Movement and the conversion of John Henry Newman in 1845 but it is the more recent and notably successful proselytising activities of Cardinal Manning which are in Matilda's mind at this time. She has seen how her beloved "rich and happy France" is "blighted by priestcraft", as she puts it in a private letter, and she uses her long and close experience of France to give weight to her warning to young England and its parents. The points she makes are familiar in her other writing. "Slavish superstition and unblushing cupidity" is her summing up of priestly religion. She anathematises what she regards as the disgraceful practices of the confessional and the horror of conventual death-in-life is given special emphasis in the experiences of Bernarde.

There is some new material in *Romance*, however, as Matilda extends the range of her anti-clericalism with vignettes of two other priests. One like Evelard is too shaken by doubt to continue in his vocation and devotes himself instead to disabusing others of outworn pieties and religious cant. The other, dim though well-intentioned, represents the narrow and thin intellectual basis of Protestantism which by the end of the novel Evelard has himself found increasingly unsatisfactory, seeing it now as merely "a stepping-stone to loftier, more magnanimous creeds". He looks forward to a time of "moral and intellectual enfranchisement" when radical rethinking will absorb the findings of science and philosophy and Darwinian evolution will be recognised as applicable to the history of ideas as it is to the development of the physical world.

Religion, or at least the clerical life, plays a big part in Victorian fiction. Pale young curates lead meek maidens to a sanctified life of child-bearing and good works, bullying rectors who care nothing for God or man dedicate themselves only to comfort and social advancement, holy men preach incessantly at home and in church and are reverenced by their mostly female parishioners. Nonconformity offers hope to the working-classes but fanatical fundamentalists preach godliness while spreading nothing but misery and despair. Novelists of all degrees of talent plough in this rich field, George Eliot and Mark Rutherford, both of whom Matilda knew, among them. When she also put questions of religion at the centre of *Half-Way* and *Romance of a French Parsonage* she was following a powerful trend but giving it a distinctive twist by the French setting and the concentration on Roman Catholicism. The implications range far wider, however, than either France or Roman Catholicism. It is religion itself which is under scrutiny and its being so reflects Matilda's own quest, evident in much of her writing, for some other basis of faith when all traditional theology is rejected. Matilda, as always, is intent on keeping herself and her books up to date with the latest thinking and in the circumstances it is a little odd that she continued to reprint until the last decade of her life poems expressing an almost childlike faith in God. Sarah Grand, close friend of later years, suggests, probably rightly, that these poems reflect "spiritual intuitions" for which Matilda was content to use old formulations though her intellectual position was certainly more sceptical and more sophisticated. Her hymns continued to be sung in nonconformist churches for years after her death.

A Romance of a French Parsonage is a serious and at times even sombre book but cheerfulness, fortunately, does from time to time break in. Matilda engages herself and her characters in intense and earnest soul-searching but she can also plant her feet firmly on the ground and treat all excess with comic irony. So she does here through the character of Georgette who lightens the tone of *A Romance of a French Parsonage* by balancing the agonised self-questionings of the principal characters with a cheerful acceptance of the less than ideal, prompted by unselfishness and a warm heart. Georgette is an older woman, a widow, who quite unashamedly confesses herself a worldling. She enjoys society and is quite unoppressed by sense of duty or theological anxiety or social theory. She believes in being happy herself and doing what she can to make others happy, giving money or her good offices to others who need them, regardless of whether or not the recipients "deserve" her bounty. This "promiscuous benevolence and unreflecting philanthropy" is not simply weak-minded, however, for Georgette is not a fool. She has her own philosophy as she explains to Bernarde. Given that human nature is faulty and society far from perfect, the only reasonable course, she has concluded, is to make the best of both rather than pine after impossible ideals. Her "religion" is similarly secular and humane, its highest aspiration being a society in which everyone would be "comfortable". The root of crime, she declares, is the "desperately uncomfortable" condition of the poor: "Better their condition, make them healthy, cheerful and contented, let good clothes, good food, innocent enjoyment be within the reach of all, and the race of criminals would be extinct in no time". It might be M. Sylvestre himself speaking. As for the after-life, she will take it as and if it comes. Death like a kind nurse will summon us to bed: "Once fast asleep, will the question disturb the wisest of us whether we wake again or no? If awakening comes, well and good. If not, the sleep will be without nightmare". She sounds much like Matilda herself on this subject and indeed Georgette's role in the novel is not a frivolous one, light-minded as she may seem in comparison with the solemn self-searchings of other characters. She stands for the affirmative vision which Matilda always recommends and it helps her in the end to an act of generosity inspired by purely human love which compares well with the sacrifices undertaken by the religiously obsessed in the name of a divinity. Georgette has for long loved Evelard and when he asks her to marry him she is happy to leave Paris and its lively social world and to share with him a humble provincial life; but when she finds that his love for Bernarde has been rekindled she gives him up without protest, though it cuts her to the heart to do so. True to her philosophy of making the best of life however harsh its disappointments, she determines not to lapse into misery but to carry on as before: "After all", she mused, "the little good done by poor creatures like myself would very likely never be done by others. There is something in that". She goes on to marry an eminent ambassador. Matilda clearly very much enjoyed Georgette. She certainly adds greatly to the humour and vitality of a book which, in spite of the ponderous characters of Evelard and Bernarde and their lucubrations, contains both. Matilda can contrive a good episode and handle it well and in so far as *Half-Way* and *The Romance* contain large-sized pills of debate and instruction they are made easy to digest with the help of comedy and invention.

Matilda continues to offer her readers further insights into French life and character in pursuit of her undeviating ambition to bring the French home to the English and make the English at home in France. A pleasantly relaxed instance of this is *A Romance of the Wire* which, published between *Half-Way* and *A Romance of a French Parsonage*, in 1891, tells a rather charming little story of French provincial life in a lightly humorous tone. Two years after *A Romance of a French Parsonage* comes a novel of different character again and, in spite of one or two successful moments, of much inferior quality. It has, nevertheless, some interest. *A Romance of Dijon* (1894) goes back in time to the early post-Revolution period which is presented as one of heartfelt enthusiasm and joy at the overthrow of the *ancien régime*. Roman Catholicism again casts its shadow over the scene but this time indirectly, through the persecution of Protestants following the Revocation of the Edict of Nantes, "that fatal action of a senile and priest-ridden despot and worn-out voluptuary", as Matilda calls it elsewhere. It was a subject of special interest to Matilda who was proud to claim Huguenot ancestry and she reverts to it a few years later in the last of the France-oriented novels, *A Close Ring* of 1907.

In *A Romance of Dijon* the theme is taken up in the person of Laurent. A Protestant like his family for generations before him, he is forbidden the open practice of his faith and is in every way discriminated against as Roman Catholicism rears its ugly head even in this, to Matilda's mind, most blessed era. Laurent becomes the protégé of Pernelle, a cousin on his mother's side, who provides him with work and later announces her intention of marrying him. There is no question of romance but she has an interest in securing his help in her business — she is a mercer — and on his side the marriage will give him position and status. Not wishing to stand in his way of advancement, Finette, the peasant girl whom he loves, marries someone else. Laurent's love affair with Finette is blighted by anti-Protestant prejudice, a malign inheritance from the past, and Pernelle likewise finds that, even in what is to her the blissful dawn of a new age, the influence of the past still lingers. Ardent revolutionary though she is, she falls in love with a dispossessed marquis and he, torn between loyalty to his class and love for Pernelle, eventually goes into exile in England and becomes a French master (at Charterhouse). The emotional quality of these two affairs, Laurent's in particular, is thin but they serve to give personal dimension to Matilda's picture of a France "standing on the top of golden hours", as the youthful Wordsworth saw it. In the end, the spirit of revolutionary France asserts itself through all personal vicissitudes and Laurent marches off as a volunteer soldier to defend the new republic against foreign invasion. The book ends, in fact, with a paean of praise to the patriotic fervour of the new France. As the call to arms sweeps through the country, Matilda evokes the separate districts with the passion of her own devotion to every part of it and the fervour of the writing becomes almost lyrical.

The book is leavened with a good deal of humour, especially in the person of Fortune. He is a mountebank, a poacher, and a smuggler who personifies in his marginal existence — and in the many scars on his body — the heartless and brutal ways of the ancien régime towards the poor — and yet, with all this, he is a fund of exuberant life, humour and wit. He stands for the vitality and resilience of the oppressed, the spirit of demotic France perhaps, but he is not merely a symbol. He has a vitality of his own and his wit and irony hold off any trace of sentimentality. Like one or two other characters from lower life in Matilda's books, he gives notice that there was a vein of sparky wit in her which in a sympathetic climate might have been given more play. Cousin Amelia also has wit and irony and a vein of satire which, at least in some of her private sketches, can be savage, but there is a quality of engaging playfulness — fun — in Matilda which when she uses it enlivens many a page in her novels. Perhaps it was an inheritance from the rural humour of farmers' parties in her Suffolk years, a legacy which Amelia did not share.

The sexlessness which afflicts all Matilda's heroines (save Kitty, exceptional in this as in other ways) combines here with French hard-headedness when material interest is at stake to produce a scene bordering on the farcical. Pernelle, the beautiful mercer, is an outstandingly efficient business-woman absolutely without sentiment — until, that is, she meets her marquis. So businesslike and unsentimental is she until that point that, when Laurent stoops to bestow a betrothal kiss, she raises her head slightly so that he can reach her cheek but she keeps on with her task of doing her accounts without troubling even to remove her pen from her mouth. She has passion, however, for her political principles. When Velours, the marquis, is recognised and in danger of a mob-lynching she intervenes single-handedly to save him, not for his own sake only but because she has a horror of seeing the glorious revolution stained by vengefulness and mob violence. To leave out the Terror in a novel glorifying the Revolution is shamelessly to air-brush history but, as Matilda treats it, the episode serves two of her causes, celebration of the revolutionary ideal and an insistent claim for recognition of the true nature and capacities of women. When Velours and his companions are seized, decent and respectable men stand back, though an atrocity is about to be committed before their eyes. They are unwilling to expose themselves to danger but Pernelle, a woman, shames them all and takes control of the situation by sheer force of personality. Matilda coins a useful phrase in her praise of Pernelle: "the absolute genuineness, the uncompromising sincerity, the legitimate manliness, so to speak, of a brave woman's nature ..."

The early days of the revolution are evoked again in *A Storm-Rent Sky* of 1898. The hero is Danton but for most of the action he is off-stage and his eventful public career merely reported. This leaves a gap at the centre which Matilda fills entertainingly enough but, without a stronger presence of the central figure, the book sags. Clearly Matilda was fascinated by Danton and she was much gratified when some years later a play based on the novel was performed in France.

The last of the "French" novels, *A Close Ring*, was published in 1907. Its subtitle, "Episodes in the Life of a French Family" describes it accurately. Politics, religion and social issues all come into the story but they are mediated through the family relationships which are the focus throughout. In this late book Matilda, no longer able to travel as she has done, looks back over her years of intimate acquaintance with French life and reflects through the novel her strongest impressions of strengths and weaknesses. The setting is Burgundy, the district closest to her heart, and the date the early 1870s when she was first forming that strong attachment to France which was to last all her life. Matilda is in reminiscent mood as she was in *Half-Way* but, twenty years later, she is past the mood of youthful exuberance. She writes again and at some length of the panther-hunter and franc-tireur of Algerian fame whose exploits Dr Bodichon used to recount and with whom she later liked to walk and talk in the woods round Dijon. He appears here as a loyal and cheerful family member, albeit a little too ready with oft-repeated stories of his adventures in earlier years. Familiar themes from her other writing about French social life reappear: the French adulation of motherhood, for example, is heroic in the mother dying of incurable disease but absurd in Marthe, whose calls for baby-worship on all occasions, momentous or trivial, are ridiculous if not exasperating. The hold of Roman Catholic superstition, as Matilda thought it, is dramatised once more in a pilgrimage to Lourdes. The scenes are described in vivid and remorseless detail, the high spirits of the rural abbés and vicars as they look forward to triumphing over science and unbelief, the pitiful sufferings and hopes of the sick and crippled and the return with hopes disappointed and no one cured. The pros and cons of the French system of arranged marriages are set out once again. Some work well but wealth- and status-hunting without feeling or respect leads to disaster. The lure of conventual life is again execrated. The central character, a hard-hearted young woman, foiled in her attempt to marry a marquis, betakes herself to a convent, not because her heart is broken nor because she is devoutly religious but simply because, in overweening pride, far from pious humility, she cannot bring herself to accept the duties and satisfactions of an "ordinary" life. She is hard-faced and stony as she says farewell to her family. She has made over all her money to the church and she refuses to make such minimal acts of charity as a gift to the dependant who has served her as chaperon, companion and secretary, or to the eleven-year-old son of her step-brother who has been left destitute. So much for the holiness of the conventual calling and of the Church which welcomes such acolytes.

A Close Ring is a retrospective novel about France and middle-class provincial French people as Matilda knew them and over the years grew to love them for their virtues and in full knowledge of their faults. As she looks back to a time some thirty years earlier, she paints a society in which the reactionary policies of Marshal MacMahon were in the ascendant, sentiment was anti-republican and the Church maintained its powerful and to her mind malevolent grip. The "close ring" of the family had itself a dark side. In good times every unit would share in its "genial shelter" but if anyone should step out of line the ring would close inexorably against the faulty one, "as in patriarchal times, the misdeed of one bringing tribal malediction". The story of Armand illustrates this. He is a young man in whom the family have invested pride and great hopes and who falls in love with Gertie, daughter of parents driven out of their native Alsace by the German occupation. The annexation of Alsace has been over the years a running sore for Matilda. It is a subject to which she has returned many times and it has a natural place in the recollections of *A Close Ring* but the emphasis in Armand's story falls rather differently from usual. That he should marry the daughter of an exiled music teacher goes against the hopes and wishes the family have for him but worse is the fact that she is of Huguenot descent. Gertie's father, speaking from sad experience, warns Armand of what the young couple must expect if they enter a mixed marriage, he a Catholic and she a Protestant. Matilda confirms the warning: "Unbelievable as it seems, in this highly polished, pre-eminently logical and amiable France, Protestants and Jews still remain a class apart. In a mixed marriage such as Armand contemplates, he will be regarded as a renegade, she as an interloper." In spite of this the young man persists in his intention and readers are left in no doubt that the road ahead for him and Gertie will be a hard one requiring all their stamina and courage. That this story of prejudice against mixed marriage harks back to the "untoward circumstances" which impeded a Burgundian romance in Matilda's own life is again a tantalising possibility.

Looking back on family life as it was when she first knew it Matilda writes with appreciation of its virtues but also with clear-sighted awareness of its less admirable aspects. The image which gives the title of the book is a telling one: a close ring which protects may also imprison and, in the France of the 1870s which Matilda describes, it is a jealous church which holds the keys. It was the free spirit of French life which always most strongly attracted her and her resentment at all that shackled and impeded it was correspondingly intense. In *France of To-day* (1892) and *Twentieth Century France* (1917) she rejoices in the reforms which have taken place, among them greater freedom for women and improvements in education which have contributed to a weakening of the church's hold on the family and social life in general. The ending of the First World War changed the world again and the life she knew passed into history just as she herself was fading away towards death. Her prescriptions, condemnations and exhortations would soon be out of date, as she had realised that sooner or later they would be. She had intended her work on France to be of use and influence in the current affairs of the day and she had expected nothing else but that it would be quickly superseded as events unrolled and situations changed. Today these books have value as social documents and also because of the personality they mirror, a woman sensitive to the physical and intellectual qualities of her environment, keenly alert to people, sometimes pugnacious in opinion, sometimes emollient, in all moods an active participant in the world about her. As for the novels on French themes, in spite of weaknesses of plot and characterisation which they share in one degree or another with the rest of her fiction, their accounts of French life in a dramatic period and of the customs and ideas which motivated and characterised it have the interest of first-hand and intimate knowledge. Matilda as novelist can be heavy-handed but she can also write well and these books retain a perhaps surprising degree of vitality and point. As an exponent of French nineteenth century life and character she has a unique place which deserves to be remembered today.

Chapter Four

THE HASTINGS YEARS

For forty years Matilda made her annual pilgrimage to France. It came to an end only when, in 1906, she had a severe illness and a breakdown which impaired her health for the rest of her life. She was no longer able to travel as frequently as she had done but she still made occasional visits abroad. Meanwhile books and articles continued to flow from her pen till the very end. She had moved out of London well before 1906, the chest problems of the 1870s having warned her that she needed to find a healthier environment, and choice had fallen on the East Sussex coastal town of Hastings, "foremost of historic towns in England", as she described it. Hastings was enjoying a high reputation as a health resort at the time and Matilda's 1906 illness and breakdown are more likely to have been due to overwork and strain than to any failure of the town's therapeutic qualities. Apart from its claims as a health resort, Hastings was also a magnet to artists and writers. Matilda already knew it through Barbara Bodichon, who lived there as a child and later built a house, Scalands, at Robertsbridge not far away. There she entertained George Eliot and, among many others, Dante Gabriel Rossetti and Elizabeth Siddal who married in Hastings in 1860. In 1873 Matilda was staying on East Parade, Hastings, and it may have been then that she met Christina Rossetti at a Scalands tea-party. "Christina was at this time about forty", she recalls, "a plainly dressed, gaunt, rather jerky woman, shy in manner and very reticent" but she said one thing that stuck in Matilda's memory: "I have never seen the sun rise in my life", she observed quietly. With her usual instinct for a telling moment Matilda did not fail to record this striking confession.

By 1883 Matilda had made several visits and knew Hastings well, as her novel, *Pearla*, testifies by its setting and evident familiarity with the town and its inhabitants, and in 1884 she took up residence in a house, Villa Julia, which was to be her home for the rest of her life. The name of the house, Matilda's choice, almost certainly commemorates Barbara Bodichon's aunt, Julia Smith, the youngest sister of Octavius Smith who was himself a close friend of Matilda's. As an active supporter of political reform and the cause of higher education for women Julia Smith was a woman to draw Matilda's admiration and affection and when at the age of eighty-four she died in 1883, shortly before Matilda moved into her new abode, it would have seemed a very suitable memorial gesture to name the house after her.

BOOKS

Women of Victorian Sussex
Their Status, Occupations & Dealings with the Law
by Helena Wojtczak
£9.99 (postage £2)

Railwaywomen
Exploitation, Betrayal and Triumph in the Workplace
by Helena Wojtczak
Hardback 384 pages. £20 (postage £5.00)

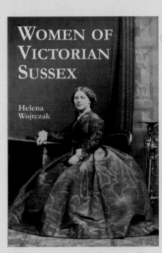

Poor Cottages and Proud Palaces
The Life and Work of Thomas Sockett of Petworth 1777-1859
by Sheila Haines and Leigh Lawson
£9.99 (postage £1.20) (Pub. late 2007)

Footplate to Footpath
The Lost Railways of the Isle of Wight
by Adrian Hancock
£12 (postage £2) (pub. Autumn 2007)

Notable Women of Victorian Sussex
A Collection of Mini-Biographies
by Val Brown & Helena Wojtczak
£9.99 (postage £2) (pub. late 2007)

Alf Cobb: Mugsborough Rebel
The Struggle for Justice in Edwardian Hastings
by Mike Matthews
£6.99 (postage £1.20)

Captain Swing in Sussex and Kent
Rural Rebellion in 1830
by Mike Matthews
£7.99 (postage £1.20)

Women's Hospitals in Brighton & Hove
The Lady Chichester & New Sussex Hospitals
by Val Brown
£7.50 (postage £1.20)

Matilda Betham-Edwards
Novelist, Travel Writer and Francophile
by Joan Rees
£9.99 (postage £1.20)

Villa Julia, still standing, is at the lower end of a terrace of houses of varied size and style, built in the earlier part of the century by a local butcher, Humphrey Wickham, who gave it his name. High Wickham, as it is called, is perched on East Hill, high above the Old Town, facing the remains of William the Conqueror's castle on West Hill and commanding a view which Matilda counted "one of the finest views in England". A journalist from *The Lady's Pictorial*, came to interview Matilda in 1891 and describes the Villa Julia as a quaint little house. It certainly fits rather oddly with its more imposing neighbours. The narrow frontage is stone faced but the side, where the front door is, reveals the redbrick structure. Matilda's sitting room was on the upper floor with a window looking out at the view. For the interior decoration she had chosen shades of gold to set off the collection of peasant pottery she had picked up in her travels and her statuettes of Goethe and Schiller which reminded her of happy days in Weimar. Watercolours, some by Barbara Bodichon, hung on the walls and there was also a small piano, "a necessity of existence" Matilda said. As to be expected, there were shelves of books in several languages and a desk at which, before age took its toll on her stamina, she wrote for five hours each morning. The five hours were later reduced to one and a half. Nothing was allowed to disturb her during those hours: "my maid does not even bring me a telegram". The dining-room was downstairs and contained old prints of Ipswich and Bury St Edmunds, Betham family portraits and an inlaid oak chest dating from 1626, a family heirloom of which she was particularly proud. It may have come from The Larches, the home that cousin Amelia shared with Mrs Braysher in Westbury-on-Trym, for on Amelia's death Matilda was given her choice of as much of the best furniture as she could accommodate.

Sharing her home was Matilda's devoted and much valued maid, Emily Morgan, who had been with her since 1874 and who stayed in attendance on her till her death. Matilda carefully provided for her in her will and Emily lived to celebrate her one-hundred-and-first birthday in the little house (Woodbine Cottage) next to Villa Julia which Matilda had bequeathed to her. Relatives still living remember Sunday afternoons in childhood when they went there to call on "Aunt Nanny". At the time of the journalist's visit to Matilda in 1891, Villa Julia was home also to a dog, a white Pomeranian, "very intelligent and affectionate", an acquisition which Matilda, an ardent animal-lover, no doubt cherished as a bonus now that she had a settled home in which to keep it. He had an identifying "necklace" with the following inscription:

My name is Muff,
That's short enough;
My home's Villa Julia,
That's slightly peculiar;
On the east side you'll find it,
With Fairlight behind it;
My missus is a poet
By this you should know it.

Matilda did not own Villa Julia and the conditions of her tenure in the earlier years cannot be traced. She told friends and neighbours that cousin Amelia bequeathed it to her when she died but there is no mention of Villa Julia in Amelia's will and indeed she never owned it. The story of the bequest is true in essence, however, if not precise in fact. Kate Bradbury (later Mrs F. L. Griffith) was a close friend who had accompanied Amelia on her American tour, was at her side during her last illness and became her executor. After Amelia's death she writes to a correspondent in America telling how she herself has bought Villa Julia out of the funds remaining from Amelia's estate when all dues have been met. She has then added it to the assets of the Chair of Archaeology in University College, London, a chair created and endowed by the provisions of Amelia's will. The gift of the house is to take effect, however, only after Matilda's death and for the rest of her life she is to be allowed to continue to live there at a peppercorn rent. (Kate Bradbury's letters were published by John William Pye in *KMT*, volume 5, 4, pp.77-81, in 1994 and are a valuable addition to Amelia's biography but unfortunately transcription of the original has produced a misleading error. What are clearly intended as references to "Miss Betham-Edwards" read in the published version as being to "Miss Bethany Edwards", a personage who exists only as a misreading or a typist's error.) In buying the house and arranging for Matilda's continued tenure Kate Bradbury must certainly have believed that she was acting in accordance with what Amelia would have wished, for she knew her better than anyone in her last years and was a close confidante. It is possible Amelia had been helping Matilda financially for some time though she herself was far from wealthy, having given up lucrative offers for further novels in order to concentrate on her Egyptological work. During her last illness she was seriously worried about money and the late granting of a Civil List pension came as a great relief. Her anxiety may have been fuelled by fear that if money for living expenses ran low, her endowment of the Chair of Archaeology would be at risk and with it her dearest wish, that Egyptology in this country should develop and flourish under the direction of Flinders Petrie, the foremost Egyptologist of his time and a valued friend. Kate Bradbury as her executor ensured that the Edwards Chair would eventually receive the maximum sum from Amelia's legacy and at the same time she made provision for Matilda. Amelia's feelings for her cousin were perhaps always in some degree protective, as in the Miss Brown episode. She praised her fiction and encouraged her poetry and may have felt some duty to act as patron to the younger woman who was bound up with happy memories of Suffolk in her own youthful days.

Matilda loved Hastings, "the picturesque, rugged, grand old fishing-town" which lay between East Hill and West Hill, but she had no sympathy with the increasing pace of developments like the new, characterless promenade, "the exact counterpart of marinas everywhere", or with modernising Philistines whose "lift" up to the castle was an offence in her eyes. At holiday times and on Sundays troops of noisy trippers were beginning to invade what Coventry Patmore called "the little, bright, surf-breathing town" but during the week peace reigned and Matilda could devote herself to her work and enjoy such socialising as she cared to undertake. There were many years of vigorous work still to be done when she first went to Hastings. She was barely fifty and retreat from London was far from implying the end of active life either as writer or traveller. Few years passed between 1884 and 1919 without the publication of at least one new volume and, though regular visits to France stopped in 1906, she still travelled. She was in Barcelona in 1889 and in France in 1909 when a play, *Danton in Arcis*, was performed in Reims, a dramatisation made by two Frenchmen of her 1898 novel, *A Storm-Rent Sky*. She was delighted by the play and its reception. To cries of "Auteur! Auteur!" she stood up proudly and bowed "beamingly" she says, to the acclamation of the audience. The play was given twice and on the second occasion the house was full to overflowing. The only known dramatic work by Matilda herself is a verse play in four acts, adapted from the German, an early piece which was published in 1861 when she was twenty-five. Apart from that, dramatic energy was reserved for the novels but in "A Pageant of Heroes", put on in Hastings in Whitsun Week, 1914, scenes, or tableaux, from *Pearla* and *Home Life in France* were represented in which, as *The Hastings and St Leonards Pictorial Advertiser* informed its readers, "children took a delightful part". Millicent Fawcett, famous campaigner for women's rights, came to the town for the occasion to honour Elizabeth Blackwell, the first woman to be admitted to the British Medical Register, who also lived in Hastings. She was warmly welcomed by the local and very active women's suffrage society but Matilda, who knew Dr Blackwell well, did not meet her.

Matilda Betham-Edwards's final home, Villa Julia, Hastings Old Town.
Photo: Adrian Hancock

Emily Morgan, Matilda Betham-Edwards's friend and helper, on her 100th birthday.
Photo courtesy of Judith Appleyard

Matilda Betham-Edwards in the Hastings years, an earlier image than that of the cover photograph which is dated 1911 when Matilda was 75.

With another vigorous campaigner for women's rights, however, Matilda initiated a close and affectionate friendship during the years at Villa Julia. She and Sarah Grand, the novelist, first met when Matilda was "upwards of sixty", i.e. in the 1890s, and Sarah some twenty years younger. Their mutual compatibility was quickly established and it is Sarah who writes the "personal sketch" which prefaces the posthumous publication of Matilda's *Mid-Victorian Memories* and which gives an intimate picture of Matilda as she lived and breathed in the last decades of her life. The immediate stimulus to their acquaintance is likely to have been the publication in 1893 of Sarah's controversial and now best-known novel, *The Heavenly Twins*, and the ensuing stir that it provoked. *The Heavenly Twins* has a cross-dressing heroine, in itself a sufficiently challenging idea for the time, and is particularly notable for its attack on the double standards whereby a woman's chastity was regarded as her most precious attribute and even the most minor infringement brought on disaster, whereas society was happy to condone the marriage of a dissolute syphilitic man to an innocent young woman. In the novel the man infects the woman and also their child and Sarah is unsparing in her account of the consequences of this hideous marriage. Whatever qualifications Matilda had about the campaign for women's suffrage, in which Sarah was an active participant, she was certainly with her in her push for greater freedom for women to exercise their energies and talents and, though men's sexual behaviour is not a subject Matilda deals with except obliquely, she would have welcomed the attack on hypocrisy and false morality. Sarah's religious views also chimed with hers, at least in their non-doctrinal basis. The religion of the future, Sarah pronounces in her novel, will "consist in the deepest reverence for moral worth, the tenderest pity for the frailties of human nature, the most profound faith in its ultimate perfectibility". With her usual zest for the latest developments in spheres where she was interested and with unabated eagerness to meet, if possible, those who were involved in them, Matilda saw an opportunity of meeting this bright young woman and seized it.

She was recovering from illness at the time in Tunbridge Wells, Sarah Grand's home-town, and she sent a message expressing her wish to call on her. Sarah, surprised by this act of condescension from a woman so much her senior both in age and professional status, made haste, as a gesture of respect, to leave her card at Matilda's hotel. She was even more surprised when a messenger from the hotel came after her with the request that she return and pay a call there and then. Sarah had forgotten, but Matilda remembered, that they had in fact met some time earlier at a public dinner when they had sat next to each other. Each had been impressed by her companion but Sarah's memory needed prompting before she could recall the picture she had formed at the time of "A bonny-looking, little elderly *gentlewoman*, with all her wits about her. Cultivated. The real thing 'old-fashioned courtesy' and all". The casual acquaintance thus renewed developed into a deep friendship and Sarah grew to love and admire "the little lady", as in the biographical sketch she likes to call her.

Matilda had, she says, the immaculate manners of "an Englishwoman of the best type" adding, in a coda which would have pleased her friend, that this Englishness was improved "by a dash of French blood and intimate association with the French themselves in France": as a consequence, she had dignity without "the stiffness and angularity which so often make English women repellent". Matilda was, she tells us, responsive and attentive to others, dainty in herself and in her surroundings. In the carefully ordered environment of her later years she reigned "like a little queen holding her court". Sarah Grand was herself a large woman —"grand Sarah", Matilda calls her — and self-conscious about the disproportion between their sizes but Matilda's smallness and her queenliness are both confirmed by the childhood memories of Sheila Kaye-Smith who became a well-known novelist, writing with a native's loyalty about Sussex just as Matilda in late novels writes about Suffolk. As a child Sheila Kaye-Smith was taken several times on visits to Matilda, an experience which she found not altogether enjoyable. Emily poured the tea outside the room and brought it in to the guests who sat round "a miniature table laid with dainty fringed napkins, tiny plates and cakes and sandwiches so minute that I found it difficult not to swallow them in a single bite". With a less juvenile appetite, Sarah Grand and other adults found Matilda's hospitality if anything over-generous and Sarah gives an altogether sympathetic account of a woman whom she found both loving and loveable. Matilda, she says, was without mannerisms, echoing in this, whether she knew it or not, George Eliot's minimal praise that Matilda had "no fringes", but with the passing of the years, Sarah has to admit, she had certainly developed a daunting number of set ways. Since her severe breakdown of 1906 Matilda had followed a restricted diet, eating only small quantities of very plain food and taking no wine except one glass of Chablis with lunch which was the main meal of her day. She took her own glass with her when she travelled. To this dietary regimen she had added other refinements and she had also become hypersensitive to noise. No sound was to be allowed in the house between six o'clock at night when she retired to her room and the hour in the morning when she awoke. A friend who was devoted and courageous enough to invite her to stay was issued with a list of requirements and prohibitions which she faithfully and anxiously observed, in the end finding herself well rewarded for the stress entailed since Matilda showed herself an entertaining and charming guest. So successful was the visit that the invitation was repeated more than once. Hastings neighbours also needed to be considerate, for notes of protest would be sent round if a piano were played too loud or too long or too late. Wartime, however, and the presence of buglers practising nearby persuaded Matilda, willy-nilly, to become less easily disturbed.

Enthusiastically gregarious as she had been for most of her life, she conserved her energies and carefully guarded her seclusion in her old age. She did not consort freely with the neighbours or other Hastings dwellers but strictly rationed her sociability. Invitations to take tea with her were regarded by the recipients with some amusement. It was like, they said, a sovereign extending the sceptre to a humble subject but they seem to have accepted that the regal exclusiveness was not a mere stand-offishness. Matilda preserved her exclusivity in age just as she resisted other pressures to disperse her energies when she was young, whether for Barbara Bodichon's good causes or in response to the blandishments of her Hungarian suitor. In age as in youth everything had to give way to the demands of the writing which she regarded as the prior commitment of her life. A photograph taken in 1911 speaks eloquently of her queenliness. Matilda sits in a chair of state dressed in rich velvet, wearing her English medal and the insignia of her French decoration. She looks out at the world with the benevolent smile of conscious if kindly superiority. There is no sign now of the "obliquity of vision" of her younger years and her firmly focused gaze looks out with the confidence of one whose title to esteem and honour she holds to be beyond doubt. The firm chin indicates will but there is a smile on the mouth and Sarah Grand judged from early portraits that Matilda's expression had softened over time, "made her eyes less brightly observant but more sympathetic". Nevertheless the glance from those eyes must always have been penetrating. Kindly she may well have been but not one to be trifled with.

The number and quality of her visitors were carefully restricted but many well-known figures found their way to her "eagle's nest". Among them was Henry James who would come from Rye and take a hackney cab from the station to Matilda's eyrie high on the hill. It was (and is) a steep climb, especially the last hundred yards or so, and many drivers insisted on sparing the horses and obliging their passengers to walk the last stretch on foot. On James's first visit the effort was almost too much for him. "He had hardly passed his prime", Matilda writes, "but [he] was ponderously built and moved with the heaviness of age" and on his arrival he had to be sat down in the ground-floor room to recover his breath, climbing the stairs to the sitting-room being obviously out of the question. Once recovered, he subjected his hostess and her surroundings to a penetrating scrutiny, the results of which were evidently satisfactory and a mutually pleasing friendship sprang up between them. "Dear Henry James!" Matilda writes in her *Mid-Victorian Memories*. "My heart glows as I recall our long, warm friendship … We valued, I may say we loved, each other, with a brotherly, sisterly affection deeper, more sympathetic perhaps than are, often, these blood relationships." They talked of France and of books and one day discussed leading women novelists of the day, Miss Braddon and Rhoda Broughton among them, to which list Henry James "gallantly" added "Miss Betham-Edwards whom I love best of all". To her disappointment the only book of hers he mentioned was the first of her novels about Suffolk, *The Lord of the Harvest*, first printed in 1899 and reissued in The World's Classics series in 1913, and of that he said merely, "I should have liked more of a tangle". He promised to send a copy of one of his own books to Emily Morgan but it was some time before it arrived and when it finally came it was accompanied by a long and more than sufficiently "tangled" letter of excuse. "Note his redundancy", Matilda remarks drily, "a couple of pages and dozens of words when two lines would have sufficed". She confides to a correspondent that she has had to send back a new Henry James novel to the publishers unread as she fears contracting his ornate style which, though delightful in him, she says, would be a disaster to others. James himself wrote about his visits to Matilda in a letter to Edith Wharton in 1909. His hostess was, he tells her, a "petite vieille" who "used to write novels [he mentions *Kitty* and *Dr Jacob*] and I used to read them, when I was young". She is now, he goes on, an officier de l'instruction publique, "rather an awful thing to be" he adds in parenthesis — "awful" presumably in the sense of awe-full — and is altogether "a very gallant mid-Victorian relic".

Distinguished outsiders apart, there was plenty of good company to choose from among fellow townspeople, including a number of distinguished women. Among them was Elizabeth Blackwell whom Matilda counted among her close women friends in the town but it is the men to whom she pays the greatest attention in her reminiscences. Rider Haggard, who presided over the dinner which honoured Kitchener, was there for a time in retreat from the harsher climate of Norfolk and William Hale White (Mark Rutherford) was for some years a near neighbour. "Gloveless, sun-burnt, homely-looking", he could at first sight be taken for a farmer, she comments, and he much resented the snobbery —"perhaps not more conspicuous in Hastings than in other health resorts" — by which he was exposed to being treated with less than due respect. He claimed a special affinity with Matilda. "If you or I had lived in times of burning alive for heresy", he said to her one day, "what crowds would be gathered there to behold the spectacle of us two at the stake". "I like Mr Hale White so much", she told a friend, "it is most refreshing to talk to him after all the *banalities* one is obliged to listen to"; but she confessed with regret that unfortunately she could hardly "wade through" his novels which she found melancholy to the point of morbidity. She makes the same complaint about Hardy.

Coventry Patmore, best known as the poet of *The Angel in the House*, was another Hastings acquaintance of long standing. Their friendship was a triumph over a chasm of deep disagreement: "Although a bottomless gulf of antipodean opinion divided us, we loved each other dearly", as Matilda puts it. Patmore was a Catholic convert — or pervert as on other occasions Matilda called those who went over to Rome. Matilda held the second Mrs Patmore responsible for this. She was herself one of Cardinal Manning's wealthiest and most devout converts and Matilda could not forgive "her beaming look of triumph" as she exulted in her success in bringing her husband within the fold. On one occasion when the two women had been discussing theological questions (unwisely one would think) Mrs Patmore sent a note to Matilda the same evening. "You will understand me", she wrote "when I say that I have more fellow-feeling with an ignorant, dirty old Breton peasant woman who belongs to my religion than with any outsider, no matter how gifted". It was hardly calculated to foster friendly feeling though, apart from her "pietistic ostentation", Matilda acknowledged her as "a very agreeable woman of the world". Patmore himself she enjoyed and admired without reservation. He liked to give people "little shocks", she says, telling his company on one occasion that, "Some of the great books of the world are coarse. Look at Othello, Dante, Calderon — who in the present time could dare to write as freely?" Equally if not more shocking was his behaviour on another occasion at a small dinner party given in Matilda's honour, when the local gentry, "squires and squiresses of the most rigid gentility", were present. As the wine was being handed round he "blurted out: 'After all that is said and done, the best drink out and out is gin and water' ". "The horrification of his guests may be imagined", Matilda goes on: "Had he turned mad on the spot they could not have shuddered more". A whole doctoral dissertation could be written on the social and economic background of this anecdote.

A particularly congenial fellow townsman was George MacDonald. He had been a Congregationalist minister but, partly for health reasons and partly because he and his congregation failed to see eye to eye on theological matters, he had retired from the ministry, adding to the number of characters, real and fictional, in whom Matilda took a particular interest on account of their withdrawal from a clerical career. MacDonald turned to literature and was celebrated as poet, preacher, lecturer and the author of numerous novels and stories for children, at least one of which, *At the Back of the North Wind*, is still remembered.

"That chivalrous prose-poet George MacDonald", Matilda calls him and he plays a major role in *Pearla* as the character Garland who, like MacDonald, is driven by the need to support a large family and becomes a prolific writer of romantic novels. Unlike MacDonald, however, Garland makes no pretence to artistic merit. He is a much loved and admirable man but, considering the difference in their literary claims and quality, MacDonald may have been less than totally happy to be associated with this self-acknowledged hack.

Matilda herself wrote for her living and like Garland she also knew what it was to be pursued by "that Fury of a romancer's life — the inexorable third volume". In *Pearla* the picture she offers is an ironic one of a writer so subdued to financial necessity that the books he writes have no merit but that they fulfil the publisher's demand for bulk. So trite is their language and so hackneyed their situations that the eldest Garland daughter has the formula off pat and when need be to meet a deadline she can pick up where her father has left off and finish his stint of pages for him.

No more than MacDonald would Matilda have classed herself with Garland but she also for most of her life depended on her pen. It did not richly reward her. Her books and articles about France had a varying reception according to the state of Anglo-French relations at the time, *France of To-Day* of 1892, for instance, being poorly received at first, whereas *Home life in France* (1905) benefited from the more friendly mood which followed the signing of the Entente Cordiale. Devotion to France enriched her life in many ways but did not line her pockets and she was driven, perforce, to make her living by writing more novels and more quickly than she should have done. Those which derive from her commitment to France have their own integrity and the six late novels based on her life in Suffolk as a girl are given depth and vitality by the personal experience and feeling involved. Many of the others, however, show only too clearly the pressure of economic necessity. Even so, Matilda would be right to repudiate identification with Garland and his ilk. Some of her books written in the Hastings years are certainly very poor — *Love and Mirage* of 1885, for instance, which was written in a comparatively fallow period when she was perhaps preoccupied with moving into Villa Julia — but total failure is rare. She wrote always with conscience, she had a repertoire of talents to draw on and her wide experience of places and events and personalities gave her plenty of scope to diversify her stories. One of her strongest attributes is her lively and alert mind and a distinctive feature of her novels, even the weakest of them, is the presence to greater or lesser degree of matter of substance, something to stimulate thought on events or ideas prominent in the contemporary world.

Forestalled, a novel of 1880 written just before the permanent move to Hastings, is a case in point. It concerns a scientist, a man who believes that science is the true light of the world which will lead mankind to "heights of spiritual and bodily felicity never yet dreamed of". His studies and experiments lead him to make a discovery of far-reaching implications which will revolutionise the accepted understanding of natural laws. As he is rejoicing in his success and the acclaim it will bring him, another man claims that he has anticipated him in his discovery and that the credit properly belongs to him. Darwin's theory of natural selection and Alfred Wallace's counter-claim to have been the first to develop it give the story a root in real life and, though Matilda goes on to wrap Norland and his rival in romantic complications and the story line wanders from France to one of the small German principalities which Matilda found so engaging, the work of a scientist and his passionate search for truth remain still the groundwork on which the rest is built. In a subsidiary development Norland experiments with the new drug, chloral, to assess its physical and psychological effects, a situation in which Matilda had a personal interest in that she had herself taken chloral during her illness of the 1870s. Scientific knowledge is again an issue in *The Curb of Honour* (1893) which turns on the subject of genetic inheritance as a crippled man, prompted by the findings of modern research, renounces the possibility of marriage to the woman he loves and who loves him lest he pass on his disability to his offspring.

The Parting of the Ways (1888) is an anti-capitalist fable in which Matilda reinforces her attack on materialist theories and capitalist economics by making the source of the principal figure's money his career as an African slave trader. Rapham (in morality-story style the names of several of the characters are significant) is immune to shame or regret and on his return to England continues his unfeeling, unimaginative way of life in which money counts for everything and all human feeling is excluded. When, however, he gets to know his daughter, whom he has not seen since she was a child, something like love is awakened in him but his nature is now too atrophied to be able to nurture it. Matilda conducts this variation on an old story with some vivacity and humour in the early stages but the "inexorable third volume" extends its deadening hand and everything is stretched too far. The filling is largely sentimental but there are interesting offshoots, a young woman, Norrie, for example, who is of an intellectual bent.

Uninterested in the usual "girlish" things, she finds her greatest pleasure in working at an invention which turns out very successfully. Everybody is astonished that a *woman* should be capable of such things. Her mother, Mrs Bee (because she is always busy) is one of Matilda's gallery of stout-hearted middle-aged women with spicy character, though she lacks the savour of some of the others.

Slavery is touched on in *The Parting of the Ways* and in a novel of the following year, *For One and the World*, it becomes a prominent motif. Characterisation is perfunctory and story incredible but again in this novel there is material to stimulate its readers to thought. The heroine, Nadine, is Russian, a fact which provides the excuse for reaction to news of the assassination of the Czar and a debate about the rights and wrongs of violence as a last resort against tyranny and oppression. Matilda is in no doubt that they should be resisted though "the accepted creeds of selfish, successful humanity", she writes, give a different message: "Let wrong get the upper hand, cruelty and injustice work their will, our first concern should be, not to get ourselves into trouble". Matilda believes differently. "There can be no doubt", she writes, "that the first duty of conscience-endowed human beings is to hate. The worst wrongs under which humanity has groaned — slavery, oppression, torture — are due to this cause, the innate laziness of the bulk of mankind, the general incapacity for hatred" — hatred to be directed, it is to be understood, not against individuals but at the principles which activate them. One of the principles ripest for hatred is slavery. The book contains a eulogy of Harriet Beecher Stowe spoken by a freed slave:

> that woman … sitting in shawl, petticoat and gown
> like any other, with a pen and a pot full of ink before
> her, did what the prophet Jeremiah and St. John on
> Patmos couldn't do, both of them put together; what
> the Bible and Testament couldn't do. She freed us
> poor slaves.

In the course of the book this man marries a pretty white maidservant, a match which meets with general approval and rejoicing among those who know them. Democratic values, the gross contrasts between rich and poor and even a prophecy of communication one day with Mars all occur within the very unsound frame of this provocative and by any literary-critical standard, preposterous — but scarcely boring — novel.

There is much indignation in *For One and the World*, not all the targets being clearly focused, but among those less bitterly identified are Americans and their dominating and noisy families: "young girls beautiful as angels, with voices as unmusical as mackaws; their fathers and others meekly submitting to filial authority". The nature and limits of parental authority is the central theme of the Hastings-based *Pearla* (1883) in which a young boy, Geoff, is to be trained to the straight and narrow by the efforts of his widowed mother and his stern tutor. Though the dead father's misdemeanours are not spelt out in detail, it is left in no doubt that his character was very far from estimable so that anxiety about the possibility of inherited weakness, moral this time, is again a concern. Geoff's upbringing is contrasted with that of his friend who later becomes his young wife. Georgie (Georgina) has the advantage of belonging to the warm and loving Garland family which is presided over by the estimable father but it cannot be said that either system of upbringing is entirely successful since Geoff and Georgie make a runaway marriage which alienates them from both families and brings grief all round until eventually reconciliations are achieved. There are, as always, delightful and amusing passages in the book but it suffers badly from the over-sentimental mother and a general aura of priggishness which is not characteristic of Matilda. The truth is that she has taken on a subject which does not suit her and which is well outside her competence. A reader coming to *Pearla* without any knowledge of her other work would be likely to conclude that she had no sense of humour and this would be a big mistake. There is humour in all the books, ranging from satire to broad comedy, and *Next of Kin Wanted*, which follows four years later, offers highly entertaining examples of them all.

The basic situation, which concerns competing claims to a legacy, is one that has served innumerable storytellers through the ages as the foundation for tales of intrigue, malice and murder but here the prevailing tone is of sympathetic amusement as the competitors each make their pitch and the conclusion is a sharing out of the booty to the satisfaction of all. When the story opens, Mrs de Robert has decided to dispose of her late husband's money and property to his next of kin as he wished (she is amply provided for on her own account) and she has put out advertisements inviting applicants. First comers are two elderly maiden ladies, Prue and Sabina, who are meek, helpless and innocent. They begin by falling into a ditch on their walk from the station to the house, having been frightened off the road by the sound of men approaching. Secondly come two Americans, the Derrobers, an older man of about sixty and his doctor nephew. The older man, "hampered" as his nephew says, "with a conscience", is a preacher. According to the younger man's account, he began by preaching against slavery before the War of Secession was even thought of "and, of course, that wouldn't do". He was put in prison and no sooner out than he began preaching against fratricidal wars with the result that he was locked up again.

"When things were settled a bit", the nephew continues, "he must needs take up the subject of political corruption. Could madness go further?" He and his nephew started a newspaper to teach "what ought to be going on" rather than report what actually *was* happening and that failed, of course. They set up an ideal community which at first "was pronounced to be a foreshadowing of the millennium itself" but that foundered. Now they want money to try once more to found "a goodly fellowship of kindred souls, work of sublime, elevating kind, recreation befitting creatures endowed with souls; and of love, neither stint nor spare" — the last item in the programme causes an agitated flutter in Prue and Sabina. What the doctor describes is a phalanstery, the ideal community of Mr Sylvestre's dream, an idea which still resonates in Matilda's mind — it makes a brief appearance also in *Pearla*. The third applicant for the de Robert inheritance is a Jesuit priest who wants particularly to inherit a Murillo painting, by the influence of which he hopes to save the souls of the heathen in the far-flung parts of the world where he is a missionary. Hostess to this company is Mrs de Robert herself, an ungracious, dogmatic, tyrannical woman who would be intolerable in real life but, contained within the comic frame as she is, she adds piquancy to the motley assembly. There has, naturally, to be a love story. The doctor falls in love with Eugenia, Mrs de Roberts' companion and protégée, but though she appreciates his intelligence and his sardonic wit she does not love him. She has long been loved by the intellectual, stern, authoritative vicar who is of a different order from the rest of the caste and stands aloof from them. His self-control and dignity as he faces the fact that Eugenia will never be his wife add a shading of near tragedy to set off more brightly the comedy elsewhere. He is counter-pointed by a comic curate, also in love with Eugenia, who is ridiculous in all he says and does: Matilda gives the vicar his due but she cannot bring herself to allow the church to escape unscathed. A late claimant to the fortune turns up in the shape of an army surgeon working on the borders of the Sahara who wants the money to help him care for orphans of "the last great famine". He is English by ancestry but a naturalised Frenchman. Mrs de Robert is quite bowled over by him and so is Eugenia: "his Gallic gaiety and openness of mind were very engaging. For the first time in her existence she had come in contact with a temperament directly the reverse of our own insular sedateness and reserve". These are recognisably Matilda's words of her own attraction to the French. The book ends with both women about to set off for Algeria and all the claimants satisfied. *Next of Kin Wanted* is a lively book with multiple comic touches but sharp also with incisive comments on life and character. Matilda's vigorous and wide-ranging intelligence is well displayed in it. The eye she casts over her *dramatis personae* is, like the doctor's, sardonic but it is also softened by human sympathy. It is striking evidence of the prevailing mood that both the phalanterist and the equally impractical Jesuit priest are allowed their sincerity and their dignity.

Matilda Betham-Edwards wrote some bad novels but she also wrote some good ones and in the worst of them there is invariably something of note. She can create the most wooden characters and involve them in the most artificial plots held together by little more than sequence but she has pictorial sense and dramatic sense and above all she is alert to the intellectual energies moving in her day and she projects them into her fictions. She sought to entertain but also to inform and to stimulate. She thought when she looked back that her choice had cost her the audience she might have had. "I think that like Joseph Conrad I have missed the public in fiction by not writing about 'ladies and gentlemen' ", she told Frederic Harrison, by which presumably she means she had not stuck within the conventional range of middle-class subjects and preoccupations. It was the "ladies and gentlemen" aspect of Mrs Humphrey Ward's *Robert Elsmere*, she thought, which had won it acclaim, especially in America, the implication being that it was because of the wider adventurings she undertook in her book that *Felicia*, though it embodied similar material, was less appreciated. She tried always to combine a challenging appeal to the forward-thinking with the romantic stories which sold popular fiction but under the pressure of the several demands she made upon herself a lastingly successful formula eluded her. Her mental and imaginative resources were, nevertheless, considerable and so to the end was her energy in mining them.

In 1899, at the age of sixty-three, with memories revived by her work on Arthur Young's *Travels* and his autobiography, she returned to her Suffolk roots and wrote, over the next seven years, six novels which drew on her experiences of farming life and farm people as she had known them in her early years. Instead of the eager following of the here and now and the big issues of the moment which had characterised so much of her work, she turned now to reminiscence and wrote with the same intimate understanding of personality and background that she had shown in *Kitty* and with the same sensitive attention to detail and nuance. Story lines protracted beyond their proper length had on occasions led her to false sentiment but the Suffolk novels are as free of sentimentality as *Kitty*. Full of affection and respect as they are, for both land and people, they are not rural idylls nor cosy dreams of a lost paradise. On the contrary, they are infused with the same energies which give buoyancy to her earlier books at their best and, coming at the end of so demanding a career as Matilda imposed on herself, they testify to a remarkable vitality of mind and imagination.

The genre of the rural novel is an appealing one. Hardy raised it to classic status and many practitioners since have explored one or more of its possibilities as historical record, as sentimental reminiscence, or as the provider of an almost infinitely adaptable background to stories of love and hate. Evocations of a lost countryside and an old way of life have perennial appeal in a world where the rhythm of the seasons and familiarity with the soil linger on, if at all, only as faint vibrations in the industrialised ether. "Our grandsires", Matilda writes, "— at least so runs the Suffolk tradition — used to prove the temperature of the land by sitting on it. If it was cold, seed-time was not come; if the contrary, the sowing began". This is the charmingly innocent side of the rural novel where simple, ignorant people follow their quaint, amusing customs and have their roots, almost literally, in the land they till; but there is a darker side. Matilda's Suffolk books acknowledge both. Such notable events in the calendar as the exuberant annual celebration of harvest-home and the colourful and noisy excitement of the occasional election are given lively and affectionate treatment with all the authority of one who was once part of the community she describes; but Matilda's novels go well beyond exercises in pleasing nostalgia. A well-honed skill in natural description, touches of lively humour and an excellent ear for local language give them a special charm but at the base is the same critical view of society and its institutions which are the bed-rock of the French novels.

The rural world of the Suffolk novels belongs to a period before the harsh times which were to follow in the mid-70s when Suffolk became one of the most depressed counties in England and the conditions of the farm-labourers were notorious; but life was hard enough earlier and Matilda states facts plainly. Stone-picking in childhood, under the merciless gaze of a supervisor, was "a system of indentured child-labour disgracing English annals". Adult life of hard labour on the land promised nothing, when strength was gone and usefulness to an employer at an end, but the harsh refuge of the workhouse. In the seasonal round, wintertime meant little or no work and "the combined miseries of cold, hunger and despair". To the weak and aged it brought "an amount of suffering … of which only eye-witnesses have an idea" (This comment comes from *The Sylvestres*, a novel which for all its continental engagement, has a Suffolk background.) The middle-class and comfortable, Matilda among them, could afford like Millison Methold in *Half-Way*, to cherish memories of "sweet Suffolk days" and "the level meadows, none fairer in England, tapestried with cowslip, wind flower and lady's smock" but Matilda did not forget that the same land presented a different face to others, as it does to Elkanah Bent, head ploughman and prominent character in *A*

Suffolk Courtship (1900). "Men like Elkanah", Matilda writes, "were wont to regard the visible world rather as a harsh and capricious taskmistress than as a smiling benevolent foster-mother. These sons of the soil endured so much for Nature's sake, how could they freely love her? Hunger-bitten hours at crow-scaring or stone-picking to begin with; later on, the long day in the fallow or harvest-field, summer sweats, winter-soakings — are such memories effaced by the sight of violet-clothed bank or wild-rose hedge?" This anti-sentimental note struck early in the sequence gives notice that, warmly as Matilda cherished memories of her farming childhood, the Suffolk books come from the same writer whose critical stance on social matters and whose reformist zeal had been well established by her writings on France.

Matilda, in fact, makes a point of reminding readers of her history as social critic and Francophile by planting references to France and the French in a number of the Suffolk books. In *The Lord of the Harvest*, for example, the earliest novel of the group, the titular hero is a simple farm worker but his story is woven in with that of his employer, Edward Flindell, whose almost equally simple soul is woken to love and sensitivity by the influence of the French governess employed at the rectory. Her favoured nationality gives her, as a matter of course, all the grace and refinement that the country people around her conspicuously lack. Believing as she did that the derogatory images projected by other writers did serious damage, Matilda was determined to use or create any opportunity to redress the balance and she did not shrink from even blatant improbability as when, again in *The Lord of the Harvest,* the Rector gratuitously informs Flindell that "we English are all loutish compared to the French. They can turn their hands — or brains — to anything".

There is considerable variety in the novels and *A Suffolk Courtship*, the novel which follows, includes, exceptionally, scenes of city life. A simple farm worker is again at the heart of the story as it opens but he fades out of central position as two other love stories, neither with a traditional happy ending, are traced. Aspects of this novel which go beyond the Suffolk background will be discussed in chapter five. *Mock Beggars' Hall*, of 1902 (it takes its name from a farmhouse in the vicinity of Westerfield), is more consistently embedded in the rural background. The central character is Naamah Forsdyke, a "farmeress" who excels in her duties as farmer and housewife and manager and who never thinks of repining at the limitations of her existence. Life on the farm is disturbed by the love affairs of her brother's illegitimate daughter, Priss (Priscilla), who lives with her, and especially by the arrival of the girl's cousin. Before his arrival Priss is courted by a rich young man and there is a remarkable scene in which Miss Ralfe, the rich young man's aunt, comes to call on Naamah. The social grace, education and refinement of Miss Ralfe overwhelm Naamah but, in addition, an intense feeling of mutual sympathy develops between the two women, in spite of the great difference in social rank, and it culminates in a kiss. To Naamah, whose life of subjection to the duties of everyday has proved "all-saving, purging the mind of unwholesome humours, keeping the body in due subjection", this experience of physical and emotional contact is a rapture as intense as any her imagination can suggest. It is a daring scene and Matilda meets the challenge head-on: "no instinct of sex comes into play", she says. The explicit rejection of any idea that lesbian feeling is at the root of the sympathy between Naamah and Miss Ralfe and the implicit assertion that women can feel warmly towards each other without any element of sexual desire entering the relationship belongs in one respect with Matilda's insistence in all contexts on women's right to express themselves without incurring suspicion or censure. It is also a personal statement with obvious relevance to her relations with her own women friends. Perhaps it has some relevance to cousin Amelia's friendships too. On any view the scene gives a powerful account of the flooding of a repressed nature by almost ungovernable emotion as Naamah's tight, narrow world is suddenly opened. Through Miss Ralfe she catches a glimpse of possibilities in life and qualities of personality quite different from anything she has ever known. "Could condescension, kindness, feeling further go?" she wonders, as she attempts to absorb this climactic experience of her life. The tightly circumscribed lives of the country-dwellers and their unquestioning acceptance of the cabined, cribbed, confined dimensions of their lives is a theme Matilda often touches on but this scene stands alone for its dramatic charge and the remarkable sensitivity and subtlety of its perceptions. She often, in different contexts, inveighs against the thwarting of inborn qualities by repressive social systems but this dramatisation of emotional starvation richly fed in one blissful moment stands alone in its imaginative power.

A Humble Lover of 1903 concerns another strong-minded woman farmer and her step-son but is chiefly notable for the introduction of an exotic figure arrived from India. She is the daughter-in-law of Mr Mingaye, an elderly, learned and, for once among Matilda's clergy, a harmless curate. She brings money and sophistication with her but most of all she brings the story of an event from her previous life when a ship she is travelling in is waylaid by pirates. In this extremity, the ship's captain makes a bargain with her: he will shoot her if the pirates win the ensuing fight, she will marry him if they are defeated. This story has nothing at all to do with Suffolk. Scarcely any book of Matilda's is quite without interest and merit but this is one of the weaker ones and something of a puzzle. With her prodigious output Matilda had no scruples about recycling material or sometimes using for padding whatever lay to hand but this is well outside her range and style. Shortage of money or perhaps creative energy may account for it. She had a breakdown in 1906 and may have been sickening for some time beforehand but *Barham Brocklebank M. D.* was published in the same year as *A Humble Lover* and that shows no lack of vigour or ambition. It may indeed have been work on that which took its toll on *A Humble Lover*.

Barham Brocklebank M. D.* is without doubt an ambitious book with every appearance of being intended as a direct challenge to Hardy by a reworking, in Matilda's own tone and temper, of one of his most famous novels, *The Mayor of Casterbridge*. Hardy's reputation as an authentic voice of rural England had irritated Matilda ever since *Far from the Madding Crowd* appeared in 1874. In Hardy's novel Bathsheba goes to the market herself with her samples of grain and negotiates with fellow-farmers, a scene which, according to Matilda, could not possibly have taken place. Anyone really familiar with farm life, she claims, would know that such an act by a woman would violate the etiquette of market-day to an extent that it was inconceivable that it could ever happen. Bailiffs or other men from the farm took grain to market on behalf of women farmers: the women themselves never. Matilda points out Hardy's "mistake" at every opportunity. No doubt she was right on the fact but she may have missed the point, for Bathsheba is a woman strong-minded enough to flout convention. Even so, Hardy may have allowed the farmers to accept her rather too easily, astounded as they are at first to see her in the market-hall. From Matilda's perspective Hardy was a rival whose credentials as a novelist of rural life were greatly over-estimated by the public. She felt, not unreasonably perhaps, that she had greater claim to the authority of intimate knowledge and, her quibble over a detail in one book apart, she criticised him more generally for his "Zolaesque" portrayals of peasant life. The first few pages of *Barham Brocklebank* strongly suggest that she was marking out her claim to the same territory and offering her own version of a Hardyesque theme.

Brocklebank is a handsome professional man of social ambition who has married his wife, Betsy, for the five thousand pounds she brings with her. The match is unhappy for she is of lower status, without much in the way of education and lacking in personal graces. He does not conceal his contempt for her and before the novel opens she has attempted to run away. In the striking opening scene he is bringing her back. He rides in his gig but to punish and humiliate her he makes her walk for an hour in a rough gated lane where she has to open all the gates as they come to them. It is a brutal scene which she never forgets and cannot forgive. Henchard's sale of his wife in *The Mayor of Casterbridge*, a similar episode of malevolence and humiliation, comes at once to mind and Henchard lies behind much of the subsequent development of Brocklebank's character. Like Henchard he is hot-tempered and lacking in any sympathy with his wife but he also has good qualities which commend him to others. He is a conscientious and much-liked doctor, always on call and treating all his patients, regardless of class, with rough good humour and kindly common sense. He rises to heroism when the local rector is struck down suddenly with cholera and nobody dares touch him for fear of contagion. Brocklebank unhesitatingly goes to his assistance, lifts him from the ground and by example shames others into giving help. From this episode his reputation grows and he becomes widely known for his success in treating cholera victims and is awarded the prestigious M. D. With his success his temptation to social climbing comes to the fore. He has no son and fixes his ambitions on the marriage prospects of his daughters. His favourite, Alicia, fulfils his hopes by contracting a very advantageous engagement but one day she thoughtlessly cuts some roses he has grown and of which he is very proud and in a spurt of the old ungovernable temper he hits her with his riding whip. She tells the rector and her betrothed's family and the disgrace of this shameful action leads to the breaking of the engagement. Alicia takes herself off to India to be a governess and her father, humiliated by his own actions and the failure of his hopes, determines to leave the town. The poor, who have always valued him, come to the house to plead with him to stay but he unexpectedly dies while they are waiting to speak to him. Obviously Brocklebank and Henchard differ greatly but there are enough similarities to suggest that Matilda was attempting her own version of a strong, deeply flawed man impelled by his nature to seek outlets beyond the scope of the rural society which constrains him. "Character is fate": Hardy quotes Novalis to sum up Henchard and the words are relevant to Brocklebank too.

Matilda herself disclaimed any reference to Hardy at all. Writing to the publisher, George Bell, in 1912 she tells him:

> Oddly enough no one has ever compared even the most tragic — i.e. Barham Brocklebank — of my Suffolk stories to Hardy and oddly enough too, excepting Far from etc. [sic] which I read when it appeared and a poor story called Two on a Tower, I have never read a line of this writer or any of his suicidally-pessimistic followers. I have never been much of a novel reader to begin with and like Mr Balfour I prefer stories that 'cheer us up'.

This may have been literally true, though Matilda's memory was not reliable in later years, but it is in any case disingenuous. Matilda certainly heard plenty of talk of Hardy and of the novel which ushered in his most powerful period. Hardy as an irritating presence on the contemporary literary scene is frequently in her mind and she does not hesitate as frequently to pass judgement on him. Whatever she had read or not read, however, and whatever the degree of influence, the fact is that *Barham Brocklebank* is a Hardyesque novel in only a superficial sense. The power of Hardy's fables and the profound poetry of his descriptions of nature are well beyond Matilda's range but the country scene is lovingly described and there are entertaining accounts of various levels of village life, Miss Tigard, for example, employed as "the finishing governess" to the rectory daughters. She has lived for two years in an ambassador's house in Paris (the acme of polish, naturally), a fact which gives her special standing in a career devoted to "Shakespeare and the musical glasses" and she has "prepared dozens of young ladies for an elegant fireside and the world". The villagers as always are skilfully drawn and in one respect this, like Matilda's other Suffolk novels, can stand direct comparison with Hardy. Profoundly ignorant as her rustics are, they have one great gift, their language and, as Matilda records it, it is one of the most enjoyable elements in her novels. These men and women cannot read but their minds are soaked in the words and stories of the Bible which they hear read in church or meeting house every Sunday and they adopt Biblical phrases and images naturally in their speech; but they are equally imbued with the day-to-day happenings and contacts of their daily lives and lively and picturesque images come spontaneously to their lips — "as safe as a tomtit on a laylock bough", for instance, or: "Kiss indeed, I'd as soon kiss a squiggling pig caught in a gate" (speaker indignant at an idea proposed in jest). Hardy's peasants with their quaint, profound or absurd commentaries on the fraught lives of their betters draw from similar sources but they speak a different language from this. Matilda's version is more down-to-earth, more convincingly realistic and no less beguiling.

With *Martha Rose, Teacher* (1906), a charming book of rural life and manners, Matilda returns to her more accustomed paths. Martha's lover, Clem, is a small farmer and therefore of a higher class than Martha whose position as teacher puts her a degree below him and only just above the rank of a labourer. Life in farming Suffolk, Matilda notes, for the humble as for the well-to-do, is as class-ridden as any in a chronically unequal society and Clem's family oppose the match. Martha is broken-hearted and Sam Wheedon, an older man who loves her, in his indignation on her behalf knocks Clem down and spends fourteen days in jail for it. In the end all comes right thanks to an act of unselfish renunciation on Sam's part when he releases her from a promise to marry him in gratitude for his standing up for her. There is Matilda's familiar touch of social protest as she points to the indifference of the squires who sit on the bench and condemn Sam to fourteen days of gruel and picking oakum with no conception of what such a sentence which they lightly pronounce really means to those who suffer it.

Love of Suffolk and its people was woven deeply into Matilda's being and could come to the surface at any time, as at the dinner-party when she and Kitchener "chatted genially on — were we not Suffolkers, knit together by an almost fraternal tie?" but Suffolk left an imprint of a different kind too. Her animosity to the Anglican church, and indeed to all institutional religion, had its roots in the sermons justifying slavery which she had heard delivered from Suffolk pulpits and she had taken indignant note, besides, of how by word and deed the clergy beat down the hopes and expectations of the poor amongst whom they lived. The rector of *The Lord of the Harvest*, for example, has no sense whatever of affinity with or responsibility for his "flock" but he is full of vigour and enthusiasm when the chance offers to lay about them with a heavy stick. The clergy bear indelibly the stigma they acquired in her early Suffolk years and they come off badly whenever Matilda introduces them. Except for poor curates, they belong to the middle or upper middle classes and as such have had the benefit of a very different kind of education from the extremely elementary kind which is all that schoolteacher Martha can offer and which perpetuates rather than bridges the gap between the social classes. Farm labourers lived in total ignorance of anything beyond their immediate experience and small farmers did not know much more. Jack Foulger, for example, of *A Suffolk Courtship* is the best farmer in the area but "the rotundity of the globe and the way this rotundity was managed" are concepts beyond his and his neighbours' capacity to grasp. "Country folk swore that the aquaeous rotundity above mentioned was brought about by a general boarding up. But such an explanation did not fit with Scripture and common sense". (The pomposity of the Latinisms, so inappropriate to those concerned, is not to be taken seriously: it is a form of witticism which Matilda likes to indulge in occasionally.) Jack determines to take advantage of the visit of a Londoner to settle the question of "how earth and water hang together". The Londoner obliges with a demonstration of the law of gravity by swinging a woman's workbasket, full of reels of cotton, tapes and items waiting to be mended, and swinging it round and round without anything dropping out. It is an amusing scene but Jack's naiveté, his desire for information and his taking it for granted that fields of knowledge exist elsewhere beyond the reach of the unsophisticated community which is all he knows, has some pathos and also a social message. Matilda has respect for the small farmers and sympathy with them and recognises that in their degree they share the disability of the farm labourers of whom she draws her most striking and sympathetic pictures.

At the base of her political views, whether in relation to Fourierism or to Marxism or to any home-grown philosophy, is her sense of wasted or stifled human potential, a sense born of observation and of her contacts with humble workers in the farms and farmhouses of Suffolk. The description of Elkanah Bent in *A Suffolk Courtship* spells out the point:

> Simple to artlessness, he yet possessed every faculty
> necessary for the fulfilment of a man's being, alas!
> such endowments for the most part lying dormant.
> These admirable Suffolk husbandmen might
> be compared to good soil, hitherto untilled and
> unenriched.

Elisha Sage, headman of farmer Edward Flindell in *The Lord of the Harvest*, is another whose nature is denied development and fulfilment. Elisha accepts, without thought of rebellion, the state of life to which he has been called but he has, all the same, a strong sense of what he owes to himself and when he purloins some grain to supplement the allowance of the farm's horses he is deeply ashamed of the loss of dignity as he is found out and humiliated. To such a nature, strong but unfocused on any object worthy of it, his relationship with the horses he works with is the powerful, central element of his life and for one horse in particular he feels a deep love. When his master is obliged to sell it, the pain of parting is heart-breaking. He cries bitter tears as he says farewell and the horse, sensing that the separation is for ever, cries too:

> from those patient yet expressive eyes fixed on his
> own so wistfully, tears now streamed plenteously also.
> The Suffolk cart-horse wept for sorrow as had done
> his immortal predecessor of Homeric story.

The scene is not a sentimental invention of Matilda's: she had seen a similar real-life parting of man and horse when both had wept and she gives an account of it in her *Anglo-French Reminiscences*. The novel's comparison with an episode of Homeric epic claims the dignity of tragedy for Elisha Sage and underlines Matilda's insistence that among the Suffolk peasantry there were souls rich in feeling and unexplored potential. That the world disregards and discards them is not their loss only but a loss to society too.

The lives of men like Elkanah Bent and Elisha Sage are constricted and crippled from birth and they accept their condition without question; but Abel Gooding, a young farmer in *A Suffolk Courtship*, wishes to spread his wings and find a place in a wider world. [There are undoubtedly once recognisable references to local individuals in the Suffolk novels and there was an Abel Gooding; but his career appears to have had no connection with his role in the novel.] The way to advancement is as firmly barred against him, however, as against Elkanah and Elisha. Abel's ambition is to get a job in government service and he presents himself for a qualifying examination. This is conducted by a man who is an Eton scholar, a Newdigate Prizeman and a Cambridge graduate, First Class, and it consists of dictation from a volume of elegant extracts. Abel, whose instruction at the local grammar school has not gone far beyond "the rudiments of reading", fails at the first word when he can't remember how to spell "government". Matilda is laying on her ironies with a trowel here and the episode is introduced quite gratuitously, having no bearing on any of the business of the novel except in so far as it reinforces the overall protest at injustices and hypocrisies which denied opportunity and development to all but the already privileged.

The lives of the women in the novels, like those of the men, are hard and strictly constrained. When Christy Kersey (*A Suffolk Courtship*) marries the head ploughman employed by her farming family, this flagrant violation of class boundaries puts her quite beyond the pale as far as family and erstwhile friends are concerned. Her story inverts the tale of King Cophetua and the beggar maid but any expectation of a romantic happy-ever-after ending which a reader may harbour is soon dismissed. Christy's married life will be one of poverty, drudgery and endless childbearing and from the start she begins to cultivate that fortitude and stoical acceptance of what cannot be changed which marks men and women alike. The women's lot is in some ways better than the men's, however, in that usually they reign supreme in the home and take charge of the money: when there is cash to spare they give their men a few pence for pocket-money. Domestic life, free of daily supervision by the farmer or his proxies which the men endure, even allows, from time to time, for unexpected talents and quiddities of character to develop. Elisha's wife, Karrenheppuch, for example, asserts her identity by composing verses and also by turning the poor health she suffers from — a consequence of the local diet of fat salted pork — into a title of honour. When the harvest is good and she has earned some money from gleaning corn, she walks seven miles each way to consult the doctor with the highest reputation in the neighbourhood. She could have gone instead to the local parish doctor but "the luxury and distinction of a doctor's bill" was a source of greater pride to her than even her reputation as a poet. Despite its narrowness, village life of the old style could breed "notable women" and in propitious circumstances native wit, down-to-earth grasp of practicalities and courageous facing of reality could develop into a pungent character of the same stock from which comes Mrs Brindle in *Half-Way*. These women at the bottom of the social scale emerge strongly as tough and resourceful characters. They, like the men, could contribute much to the world were they only given the chance to develop their capacities. As for the "farmeresses", women like Kezia Kersey in *A Suffolk Courtship* and Naamah Forsdyke in *Mock Beggars' Hall*, they are efficient, strong-minded women who run their farms with total competence and authority but they also accept without question the narrow, pinched lives they have been born to. Some in the younger generation are becoming less passive and kick against the traces, like Priss in *Mock Beggars' Hall*. She has a zest for a brighter life and for adventure but she has little hope of either in England and takes herself off with her lover to that famed land of opportunity, America. Amma in *The Lord of the Harvest* is another independent-minded young woman also very hard-headed: "Before the realist novel was thought of, Amma regarded existence from the realistic novelist's point of view". This is a remark which bodes ill for Amma, since Matilda considered that the realistic novel took a blinkered view of life. It was not realistic enough, she said. Sure enough, Priss by misjudged stubbornness loses a chance of happiness and condemns herself to an unsatisfactory marriage.

A feature of the Suffolk novels which is conspicuously absent elsewhere is the acknowledgement of sexuality. As an element in the feeling which grows between Naamah and Miss Ralfe it is explicitly denied by Matilda but in other novels even the young women who will eventually marry their suitors are excluded from any awareness of physical desire. Matilda did not write "ladies and gentlemen" novels but she could not breach the proprieties of the drawing-room if she wished to be accepted and many a false note in the novels arises out of enforced prudery. In Suffolk, however, things are different. The young men and women of the kitchen and the farmyard are allowed passionate kisses and may only be saved at the last moment from going further. Young women who have "made a mistake" are received without opprobrium as servants. Priss, the illegitimate child of her brother, is accepted as a full member of the family into Naamah's household. Indeed it could hardly be otherwise. Matilda is too sensible and knows her country people too well to attribute the manners and morals of the middle class to young Suffolkers living an arduous physical life close to the soil. It is only a pity that she could not use the same freedom elsewhere.

Chapter Five

BITTER SWEET

Matilda suffered a stroke on December 8th, 1918, and died a few weeks later on January 4th, 1919. Her last message to Sarah Grand was that she was quite cheerful, and meant to keep up her spirits to the end. The instructions she gives in her will are clear-headed and firm. She was to be cremated "at the least possible expense" and a Theistic or Unitarian service was to be held at the crematorium. No flowers were to be sent, there was to be no tolling of bells and no memorial service. She appointed Clement Shorter, friend and well-known editor and critic, as her literary executor. Emily Morgan, who served her devotedly for forty-five years, has priority among the bequests and is carefully provided for with an annuity, a cottage, and items of household furniture. Suffolk has next call on the legacy and Ipswich Museum receives the precious oak chest, engravings, family portraits and other items associated with the Suffolk years, as well as two French diplomas, the 1908 medal and the French decoration. Hastings Museum receives the collection of pottery garnered in Matilda's travels together with books, pictures and other items. Matilda would have been galled to know that the museum rejected some of these items as not suitable for display and returned them to her executor. There are individual bequests of small sums of money and personal mementoes to friends and Betham relatives. Five pounds is left to a friend to be used for the benefit of the poor. Her estate was valued at slightly over eight hundred pounds. Amelia's was valued at three thousand, a considerably larger sum than Matilda's, but hardly a fortune. Bequests in Amelia's will include one hundred pounds to Matilda.

On January 11th *The Hastings and St. Leonards Observer* published an obituary written by a High Wickham neighbour, Thomas Parkin, in which he refers to a letter sent by command of Edward VII to express appreciation of her work in forwarding Anglo-French entente and to George V's having "graciously accepted" an autograph copy of her book, *Hearts of Alsace* (1916). The information presumably came from Matilda herself though she makes no reference to these royal acknowledgements elsewhere. In October 1920 a memorial tablet was placed on the front of Villa Julia recording her occupancy. An earlier suggestion that a plaque should be put up in her lifetime had been dismissed with horror by Matilda who was by that time inflexible in her determination to reserve personal access to the select few. At her funeral only the author of the obituary and an old friend were present, together with her solicitor and executor, Archibald Edward Young, whom Frederic Harrison describes, in a letter to John Murray on February 9th, as Matilda's nephew. There is no other evidence of this relationship but Matilda's will is careful to ensure that Young is indemnified for his responsibilities both as executor and solicitor and personal bequests are made to him and to his daughter, suggesting that there may have been a family connection. The firm of Young, Coles and Langdon, solicitors, is still conducting its business in Hastings today.

The Times obituary was written probably by Sir Sidney Lee, editor of the Dictionary of National Biography. It traces the outline of her life and credits her "with no inconsiderable popularity as a novelist" (though it adds that "her fiction lacked the highest distinction"). It throws the main emphasis on her French writing: "she became an interpreter of France and the French to England and the English... her enthusiasm, her humour, and her definite point of view" distinguishing her as the most interesting among contemporary commentators on France.

Matilda's will with its emphasis on economy in the funeral expenses and the modesty of the bequests leaves no doubt that her lifetime of writing had been poorly rewarded financially. She had been her own agent and in placing her French work and negotiating terms she had been more eager to put her thoughts and findings before the public than to press for money. It was "a labour of love" as she several times says and as she says too in respect of the considerable researches she did in preparing her edition of Arthur Young's *Travels* and his autobiography. She reminds publishers from time to time to send her a cheque when funds are running low and is grateful when occasionally they add to the sum originally promised. As a popular novelist she could not compete in sales with the likes of Charlotte M. Yonge or — more to her taste — Mary Elizabeth Braddon, about whom she wrote admiringly, but her books were widely read and disseminated. Before publication in book form many were serialised both in this country and America and in 1911 Tauchnitz held thirty of her novels. German and French translations were popular but editions in general were cheap and returns were evidently small. In 1907 friends and admirers presented her with a silver inkstand which is now in Hastings Museum. As the inscription on it notes, it was a gift to mark her literary jubilee, the fifty years that had passed since the first publication of her first novel, *The White House by the Sea*. On the same occasion, as the inscription also records, they presented her with a cheque for two hundred pounds. This, and a legacy of three hundred left to her in 1887 by a wealthy Hastings citizen, may indicate that her relative indigence was well known among her acquaintance.

However this may be, Matilda remained buoyant to the end and she had her triumphs. In July 1911 she received a cheque from Tauchnitz for *The White House by the Sea*, still being published so long after its first appearance: "How many dazzling reputations have vanished meanwhile!" as she gloatingly exclaimed. She was devoting herself with enthusiasm to revising her French books for reissue, adding new material as needed to take account of fresh information. "All these books are as bread cast on the waters", she says, "seen after many days bringing in a little money". In 1913 she told Frederic Harrison that she was "very much alive" and in 1916 claimed that she was "still much in demand". For several years she wrote autobiographical sketches and short stories for the *Cornhill Magazine* and these were gathered together and published as a book, *From an Islington Window*, in 1914. With a mixture of gratification and some ruefulness, she reports to Clement Shorter that it is "more praised than any work of fiction I wrote in my heyday!!" Publishers alert to the publicity value of her longevity were taking a fresh interest in her and Smith, Elder, who published *The White House* in 1857, went so far as to ask for a new novel to mark her sixty-year Diamond Jubilee. At first she says she is too old to undertake it but the temptation was irresistible and she wrote *Hearts of Alsace*, featuring Mlle. Petry, a perky brave shopkeeper who defies the Germans with good humour and ingenuity. She is one of a group of delightful older women who occur from time to time throughout Matilda's career and light up the books in which they appear. This is the book which George V "graciously received" and it seems to have kindled in Matilda fresh enthusiasm for even more work. In a letter of March 1918 quoted by Sarah Grand she writes that she is "just finishing a set of fire-eating short stories (autobiographical) of Germany and France. If the Huns get here I shall be shot, that's certain"; but these stories appear not to have survived. She was also working on a new novel and had plans for yet another.

Money never flowed freely but she was awarded a Civil List pension on the recommendation of Sir Arthur Spurgeon and in the end was comfortable enough to be able to tell the publisher, George Bell, that she was in easy circumstances: "at any rate I do not at all depend on literary earnings ... fortunately", she adds, "I have no one belonging to me in needy circumstances". For a volume of translations of *French Fireside Poetry* with notes, she asks for no payment for this was another "labour of love". It appeared in 1919. One particularly bright spot in the late years gave her immense satisfaction. This was the republication of *The Lord of the Harvest* in 1913 in the Oxford World's Classics series. To be admitted to this most prestigious list by the "best press in the world" was an honour which gave her, after years of ill paid work for cheap publication, almost inexpressible delight. Adding to the joy was the fact that Frederic Harrison had agreed to write a foreword. Harrison was an *eminence grise* of the late Victorian period, a lawyer by training, a critic and biographer and the leader of the Positivist movement in England. Matilda had known of him and admired him for many years but met him for the first time in July, 1890, as he recalls in a letter printed in *Mid-Victorian Memories*. It is typical of her eagerness to make first-hand acquaintance with notable and interesting figures that Matilda had invited herself to visit the Harrisons in their cottage in Sussex and Harrison remembers the moment when he handed out of the coach "a bright and smiling lady who seemed to be on the right side of fifty". In fact she was fifty-four. "It was love", he goes on, "— i.e. lifelong friendship — at first sight, and we have been lovers, in the sense of close and intimate friends in thought ever since". They corresponded with each other thereafter till the end of her life, discussing books, current affairs, mutual friends and personal matters concerning his family or her publishing fortunes. He tried to persuade Matilda to join the Positivists but, as always, she refused to commit herself to them or any other group: "I have never so much as joined a Ladies' Committee," she tells him. Nevertheless there is much in Positivism which she admires, as she explains: "having waged inner war against obscurantism since I first thought at all, it is with your body that I have felt most sympathy." It is a mark of their confidence in each other that in 1907, after commenting admiringly on two of her Suffolk novels, he is able to advise her that she should never write another line. "You have rather weakened your fame by writing so much", he says boldly. As for money, a life annuity, he tells her, would bring her in much more money than she could make by her pen. It was good advice and up to a point she took it, in the main restricting herself to revising previous work and drawing further on her reminiscences. She could not entirely stop writing. Her brain was too active and her ambition still too much alive and the money, in any case, was still very welcome.

Harrison was long familiar with Matilda's writings about France but he came to her novels late and was at once captivated by *Kitty* which he admired whole-heartedly. As for *The Lord of the Harvest*, it was, he told her, "more interesting and a finer and broader study of real life than *The Mill on the Floss*" and he blamed himself for not having realised earlier her quality as novelist and drawn greater public attention to it. The preface he wrote for *The Lord of the Harvest* stresses the pastoral innocence of the world it describes, "this delicious idyll" he calls it, by, as he grandly dubs Matilda, "the *doyenne* of our English novelists". He is tempted to enter on a comparison between times then and times now: "Was England, say in 1843, a land less happy in a high sense, less great, less religious, less humane, than it is in 1913?" but drags himself back to extol Matilda's familiar acquaintance with folk ways, her sympathetic use of local idiom and the "patriotic glow" with which she depicts the Suffolk countryside. Matilda had good reason to be pleased. She sincerely admired Harrison and highly valued his opinion and she believed that his endorsement would give an invaluable fillip to her status as a fiction writer. The review gives a tempting taste of the contents of the book and she well knew that endorsement by a known and respected figure could do wonders for a book's and a writer's reputation and, incidentally, for sales.

Harrison was not present at Matilda's funeral and after her death he wrote a somewhat bad-tempered letter to John Murray in which he refused what appears to have been a request to write a biographical note introducing *Mid-Victorian Memories*, the volume of reminiscences which Matilda was preparing in her last months but which she did not see into print. He states, surprisingly, that he had met her only two or three times and he denies knowing her novels. Since he refers to at least four of them in his letters this is evidently a lapse of memory of the kind which he suspects may lately have befallen her. He is referring to the possible use in the *Memories* of some of his letters to her. He has given permission for letters to be used but asks to see the relevant pages before the book goes to print so that he can check that Matilda has not forgotten, misread or otherwise misinterpreted his intentions. Unfortunately, the request came too late. The book was in print and when Harrison saw it he was enraged to find that his "confidential and often playful" letters, "such as he never contemplated leaving the hands of his old friend", were included. Harrison had already proved himself highly sensitive to publication of any part of his correspondence on whatever excuse and had on an earlier occasion reproved Matilda for a minor breach of his embargo. He insisted now that copies of the *Memories* should be prefaced by a publisher's note to the effect that "by an unfortunate misunderstanding" letters from him had been published without his consent. Whose memory was at fault, which of them was confused about the agreement in respect of the letters in *Mid-Victorian Memories* are questions beyond settling. Whatever the facts, it is a pity that this last volume should be marred by a blot on its opening page and especially a pity that it should be due to Harrison whom Matilda so much admired and whose friendship she so highly valued. Fortunately she did not live to see it.

Harrison may have written her obituary for *The Positivist Review* before he saw the offending volume of *Memories* but it is, in any case, a fair account if lacking in warmth and not entirely accurate. He had expressed the highest admiration for *Kitty* to Matilda herself but here he merely mentions it among others and singles out *A Suffolk Courtship*, *The Lord of the Harvest* and *Mock Beggars' Hall* for special praise as historic records of "Old England" before the repeal of the Corn Law. He had encouraged Matilda to believe that the best of her work would keep her name as novelist alive for at least a hundred years: "You will be read with delight in 2013", he told her but in the obituary he, like *The Times* obituarist, puts his emphasis on her French work. Both gentlemen, perhaps, felt it more becoming to their own dignity to concentrate on studies of the social fabric in an international framework rather than risk suggesting that they were in any degree connoisseurs of fiction. Matilda, for her part, hoped and believed that her French work was of substantial value for the time when it was written but she quite well knew that its usefulness would inevitably soon depreciate as time passed and situations changed. She pinned her hopes of lasting fame on *Kitty* and, after Harrison had given it the benefit of his blessing, *The Lord of the Harvest*. She might have been disappointed by the balance of the obituaries.

Bitter Sweet was the title of a novel with which, in the months before she died, Matilda was planning to make a positively last appearance as a novelist. It is a suitable one for an assessment of Matilda's life and career. The picture of Matilda in old age is a mixed one. She was loved by some, admired by many, had good friends, lived in modest comfort and was not harassed by shortage of money. Her health was never robust after her severe illness of the 70s and again in 1906 but later years were free of serious health problems and she prided herself on retaining her faculties unimpaired. Reprints and calls for more work gave her a pleasant flurry in the very last years and assured her that the world regarded her and recognised her work. On the other hand she had an obsessive sense that she had not had her due and as late as 1918, in spite of many testimonies of respect, she was writing to Sarah Grand:

> My literary Diamond Jubilee 1857-1918 won't I fear, bring me my deserts, viz., the title of Baroness as accorded to Miss Burdett-Coutts. Any lesser distinction I should refuse, as these are showered upon grocers, bakers and candlestick makers.

This may have been written, as Sarah Grand assumes, "with a wry smile" but it accurately expressed her bitterness at the lack of public recognition in her own country for what Sarah Grand with justice calls "some of the best works ever written on French life, organisation and character." She had been much offended when on the occasion of a visit of French dignitaries to London in 1911/12 no invitation had been given to her and she took such neglect as symptomatic of the failure of British society in general to appreciate women's work. They ordered things better in France where she had been signally honoured. Matilda tells how a French visitor whom she was conducting round Westminster Abbey was astonished to see that Poets' Corner contained no memorial to George Eliot, or Charlotte Bronte, Elizabeth Barrett Browning or any other woman of the period except Jenny Lind — and Jenny Lind was a foreigner, given her place by personal intervention of Queen Victoria. The Queen's opinion that suffragettes ought to be whipped tells clearly enough of the limits of her sympathies with women's movements.

As for Matilda's own views of women's claims to exercise the vote, they hardened over the years in reflection of the bitterness which in some moods overcame her. In *Anglo-French Reminiscences* of 1898 with her Suffolk experiences in mind, she offered as "a capital argument on behalf of female suffrage" the refusal of some landlords to grant renewal of a lease to widows, sisters and daughters of deceased tenants because the landlords wanted the property represented in Parliament. Rate paying and the vote, Matilda argued, should go together:

> Why they [women] should manfully [note the word] keep the world a-going, support Her Majesty's soldiers and sailors, contribute to Colonial expansion, yet, like the occupants of the Oriental harem, be subject to masculine law-making, has ever seemed to me to be opposed to common sense and the most elementary notions of justice.

She was and remained vehement about the arbitrary restrictions imposed on women which denied them the full expression of their natures and their talents but as time went on she became increasingly cynical about the qualities and capacities of her sex. "Women are very disloyal to each other", she writes in *Mid-Victorian Memories*. No Girtonian has troubled herself to write a biography of Barbara Bodichon, "the noble foundress" to whom she owes so much, nor has any woman produced a biography of Amelia Edwards, "the erudite explorer in recondite literary fields", a somewhat strange description of her cousin's career as an Egyptologist. "In advancing years", she concludes with devastating finality, "I am more and more struck with the littleness and self-seeking of my sex, and less and less desirous of seeing them either in Parliament or holding any public office of responsibility whatever". This mood of bitter rejection of women's aspirations to political equality and the blanket disparagement of their qualities sits ill with her respect for the distinguished women she has known and, most immediately, with her friendship with Sarah Grand of whose fight for female suffrage she certainly knew. It is clearly a reflection in a bad hour of her sense of neglect and of resentment at being denied the degree of public recognition she felt was her due.

Such feelings burst disconcertingly into open expression at least once. Sarah Grand recalls the embarrassment on a domestic occasion when Matilda's friend and doctor, James Hessey, took too much interest for her liking in the recently published work of a fellow guest: "Never have you said so much about any one of my books!" the hostess exclaimed. She was generous and helpful to novice authors and Sarah Grand says that she rejoiced in the success of others but a streak of animosity pushes itself irrepressibly into view when she feels her own work threatened or diminished. She attempts to dismiss Hardy, her rival in the rural novel, and she makes passing snide remarks about Du Maurier, whose highly successful novel *Trilby* poaches on her French territory.

These are no more than small and pardonable weaknesses, hardly unexpected or unusual in a competitive environment. What is much more surprising, however, even astonishing, is a burst of bitter animosity directed at cousin Amelia eight years after her death. The potentiality for discord and outright irritation between the cousins had always been present, as for example in Matilda's adoption of a B (Betham) in her name to match Amelia's B for Blandford, thereby causing unnecessary confusion in attributing their books, but nothing prepares for the nature and force of the hostility which finds expression in the second Suffolk novel, *A Suffolk Courtship*, published in 1900. During the preceding ten years Matilda's hard work on Arthur Young's *Travels* and autobiography had taken her back to Suffolk both in mind and in fact and it had stirred old memories of people and places of the past. The six Suffolk novels written between 1899 and 1906 owe their existence to these revived memories but it was not only her rural background which came fresh to Matilda's mind as she returned to old haunts and old interests. Intimate personal recollections which had been buried for years under the preoccupations of her maturity now came to the fore, among them vivid recall of the impact of first acquaintance with cousin Amelia when they were both children. With this flood of memory came also sharpened consciousness of the different courses their subsequent careers had taken and the always more glowing reception Amelia had received from childhood on.

Roots of the jealousy which springs into full growth in *A Suffolk Courtship* are discernible with hindsight in the *New England Magazine* article of January 1893 which was written as a memorial essay. The young Amelia, "the personification of fun and childish daring", who on her first appearance hurls the nursery loaf out of the window for a bet, was evidently a handful and, the article implies, was being spoilt by her doting mother. Mrs Edwards, full of pride in her gifted daughter, never tired of heaping praise upon her, even in young Amelia's hearing. "The achievements of the youthful story-teller, artist and musician were freely vaunted in her presence", Matilda writes with evident disapproval. Others paid a price for this adulation and maternal indulgence. Full of energy and unchecked high spirits Amelia one day drained away half a cask of harvest beer, the much-prized champagne of the countryside — it was evidently a thoughtless joke — and at another time she locked the admirable Aunt Maria in a pantry. There was no knowing what this formidable girl would be up to next but aunts and uncles were schooled to bear it all patiently. "The escapades were overlooked on account of the phenomenal acquirements of their niece", Matilda writes. "A child who had gained the prize for a story at nine years of age [as Amelia had] could hardly be expected to behave as others". A note of irony, if not outright disapproval, sounds in all this but Matilda does not neglect to pay generous tribute on her own account to Amelia's gifts and what she herself gained from her example and her influence in those early days. It was Amelia who gave her her first piano lessons and she, like the rest of the family, profited from her literary taste and the readings of Shakespeare and other poets which she gave to a family audience. Everyone was impressed when on the walls of a box room at Creeting St Peter's, home of Uncle William and Aunt Maria, Amelia designed and drew in black chalk a six-foot wide cartoon of "The Landing of the Normans in Britain" but, among these positives, Matilda also remembers her fright when Amelia woke her roughly one night from a deep sleep to test her memory of a poem by Keats, a somewhat unkind tease it would seem. Thoughtless indulgence of her own high spirits at some expense to others is hinted at again in an anecdote of the pleasure Amelia took a few years later when she dressed up in male costume and presented herself to the bewildered family as a young man from London. In a brief chapter on Amelia in *Mid-Victorian Memories* Matilda returns to this and perhaps other similar charades of her irrepressible cousin: "Nothing delighted her so much as camouflage, in other words, taking people in; as we Suffolkers say, making them look a gaby". Rather than enjoyment of ingenuity and skill in performance, Matilda's words suggest something close to dislike. Here and elsewhere admiration struggles with annoyance. Matilda could not and did not at any stage wish to minimise Amelia's gifts but irritation at the praise she received and envy of her accomplishments were implanted in childhood and could not be eradicated. In time the seed thus planted produced in *A Suffolk Courtship* a poisoned flower.

    A Suffolk Courtship is a remarkable book on several counts. It shocked Frederic Harrison when he read it, though he did not pick up the hinterland of personal reference. He thought it as good as *The Lord of the Harvest* but he recoiled from what he found its "fearfully pessimistic" tone. Readers would reject it, he told Matilda, as a picture of "too gritty and heartless a world down in Suffolk farms and your insight into their hearts — or say their insides — is too cynical". Sentiment, passion, "something ideal" is much more palatable, he tells her. Matilda did not need to be told this. Tough though her material had sometimes been she had always kept one eye on the delicate sensibilities of her audience, a fact which makes the overall tone of *A Suffolk Courtship* all the more remarkable. There are attractive rural scenes and some amusing episodes but a mood of cynicism, disillusion and disappointment runs throughout the novel, whether the focus is on Chrissy's marriage to Elkanah or Abel Gooding's ambition to rise above his rural limits or, a third story, the pampered youngest Kersey sister's hopes as she prepares to embark for New Zealand with her new husband. The man is ignorant of farming matters but expects to take over a large land holding and make a good living from it and for her part Susie dreams of queening it in a new and open society where she can flaunt her boarding-school manners and her smattering of education. Neither has any conception of the realities of emigrant life in store for them. To put it beyond doubt that their life will be hard beyond their imagination and that all their hopes will blasted, the land tenure they rely on has been guaranteed by a bishop, a fact which, given Matilda's view of churches and their ministers, adds the last bleak touch to their future: they are sure to be cheated and fleeced. Emigration was the resort of many who could find no place in their native country and Matilda, like other novelists of the time, uses it more than once as a hopeful ending to stories of defeat and frustration. *In A Suffolk Courtship* it is presented to the contrary as a snare and a delusion and Matilda seems to take positively cruel pleasure in heightening the irony of innocent hopes.

Irony, in fact, ranging from the bitter to the comic, is the key weapon by which Matilda explodes the various illusions at play in this novel. The title suggests that the book will be the story of one courtship but in fact there are several, including Jack Foulger's honest but unrewarded wooing of the eldest sister, as well as the weddings of Chrissy and Susie. There is also the love-life of Abel Gooding, who first directs his attentions to Susie and then, because of the disgrace of her sister's marriage to a farm-hand, withdraws them. She tries to act the part of a deserted lover according to the prescriptions of romantic novels and flings herself into the duck pond; but Elkanah (the indirect cause of Abel's faithlessness) unglamorously fishes her out. She then tries to waste away but a life of mooning around listlessly and waiting to die proves too boring. At this point she meets the man who will take her to New Zealand.

Meanwhile Abel has been captivated by a stranger from London who has burst on to the country scene with dramatic and disruptive effect. The stranger is a striking young woman whose real name is Martha but she prefers to be known by the more glamorous "Inez" — she has been for a time a governess in Spain. She and her mother, Mrs Als, have come into the country in temporary retreat from their London home, bringing with them all that is antagonistic to the rural life they invade. Their first entrance, battering at the door of a farm where a Christmas dance is being held and insisting on being admitted, is typical of their unsympathetic intrusion into a relatively innocent and unsophisticated community. Full of pretension, they boast of their London background and despise the country people into whose lives they have forced themselves. "What a set of clod-hoppers", Mrs Als remarks to her daughter. Both of them cockneys, born within the sound of Bow Bells, they much prefer gaslight, bustle and excitement to the beauties of nature. They are keen theatre goers and light comedy at their pet minor theatre or the last new comic song and a display of fireworks at Vauxhall are more to their taste than anything the countryside offers. Inez herself is a gifted performer in amateur theatricals and in this as in other things she amuses herself by parading her superior accomplishments and airing her pretension to metropolitan polish.

In her various talents, her manner of speech, her distinctive laugh and, above all, her power of irresistible attraction which draws admirers to her, a reader with some background knowledge of Matilda and her connections will gradually realise with increasing amazement that the figure of Inez is, in fact, a grotesque parody of cousin Amelia, Amelia with all her shining attributes turned, as it were, inside out and made ugly. As she is travestied, so is her mother in the person of Mrs Als (Mrs Edward's first name was Alicia). In the *New England* article Mrs Edwards is a "brilliant complexioned, bright-eyed, large-featured little Irish woman", clever and lively by temperament. In the novel she becomes "a short, dumpy, middle-aged duenna, with the round, rubicund, unmistakeable face of a bonvivant, an enjoyer, one to whom nothing in the way of pleasure, from a pantomime to a pippin, came amiss". The lively nature noted in the article is now construed as vulgarity. The strong attachment between Amelia and her mother, emphasised on other occasions, becomes in the novel a heartless disregard of the husband and father who is excluded from their companionship. The figure of Mr Als exactly duplicates the figure of Mr Edwards as portrayed in the *New England* article but whereas he is given dignity in the article he becomes a pitiable figure in the novel.

If there is any doubt about the originals of the Als family it is dispelled when they move to London. The Als's live in what Inez describes to Abel as "a retired and very select little street leading off the City Road and within reach of many attractions — the New River, Sadler's Wells and an excellent minor theatre almost at our doors". Abel is not in a position to know that the "retired and select little street" is not, in fact, the well-to-do environment which Inez with her usual self-aggrandisement gives him to suppose but a far from prosperous area inhabited by small traders and clerks. To pinpoint it exactly, Matilda gives the Als's actual address, 1,Westmoreland Place, City Road.

This is the house where Amelia was born and the Edwards's lived until they were eventually able to move to a pleasanter location in Wharton Street, Percy Circus. Unattractive as the Westmoreland Place house may have been, the young Matilda was glad to spend her evenings there during her unhappy months at the seminary in Peckham. There the Mr Als of the novel, a sad and lonely figure, leads a monotonous and cheerless existence, circumscribed and unvaried on precisely the same pattern as that of Amelia's father as described by Matilda in her article and elsewhere. Only in the novel is it suggested that the limitations of this narrow and over-regulated life were owing in any part to the coldness and neglect of the much younger wife and the daughter who was her chosen companion. "Not that Inez could be accused of unkindness", Matilda writes, "but from babyhood she seemed her mother's sole possession, only his so far as cost of bringing up was concerned". Favoured with no more than token recognition by wife and daughter, the father has to rely on an unmarried brother and sister, small dairy farmers whom he visits each year during his annual vacation, for the moments when he is able to "warm himself in the dim sunshine of feeling". Mr Edwards in real life took his annual vacations in visiting unmarried brothers and sisters on their farms. To blacken the situation further in the novel, cholera breaks out in London and Inez and her mother take refuge in the country. There they give themselves up to enjoyment, untroubled by anxiety about the husband and father whose work obliges him to stay in London. He contracts the disease and dies alone and uncared for except by a faithful servant. The basis of fact in this story is that a cholera epidemic did break out in London in 1854 and Mrs Edwards and Amelia did retreat to Suffolk; but Mr Edwards did not die then. He lived till 1860 when he and his wife died within a week of each other. The *New England Magazine* article confirms that during the cholera epidemic the twenty-three-year-old Amelia did make the most of the unplanned opportunity to return to the country and the company of young relatives. "Perhaps Amy never spent happier, more careless days", Matilda writes: "She rode, drove, rambled, rusticated, the life and idol of the party" — she is still evidently the dazzling cousin who invades Matilda's home territory and becomes once more the focus of everybody's attention just as she was as a child. The article suggests no criticism of her behaviour but the novel is unsparing in contempt for the thoughtless, heartless behaviour of both Inez and her mother while the fictional father is dying alone and neglected in London. Here as elsewhere, the novel and Matilda's witness on other occasions present two versions of the same behaviour and, with significant variants, the same events, one sympathetic and even laudatory, the other hostile and even vicious. The question is: why so virulent and why at this date?

The jealousy of a child resenting the adulation offered to another is understandable. Young Amelia bursting with talent and energy, may well have been too full of herself and too full of life to be aware of the feelings of one of the youngest of her cousins who was relegated to the wings while she occupied centre stage. She and her mother may have been less than tactful on their first acquaintance with country manners and country customs and perhaps betrayed amusement or even some scorn. Amelia, familiar only with the lilacs and laburnums growing in the tiny city gardens of the Islington she knew, may have needed time to appreciate the subtler beauties of the Suffolk countryside though, if so, she made up for it afterwards, paying at least one nostalgic visit and including warm memories of it in her novel, *Barbara's History*. Perhaps she revelled a little thoughtlessly in the unexpected pleasure of return to Suffolk during the cholera outbreak but at the time she was under the strain of a broken engagement and an uncertain future. That she and her mother were very closely in sympathy with each other is certainly true and the father may in fact have been to some extent excluded but Amelia respected him and was proud to display his miniature and his Peninsular medal in a place of honour in her study. Thomas Edwards had, "oddly enough", as Matilda remarked, made friends with an enemy officer during the campaign and received a ring from him which Amelia in turn gave to Matilda, knowing that her cousin would specially value it as, in Matilda's words, "a precursor of an Entente Cordiale as yet undreamed of by the most Utopian". Such details leave open the real nature of the family relationships but the unrelieved animosity of the treatment of Amelia and her mother throughout the novel puts the worst possible interpretation on every situation. Matilda lost her own mother while she was still a child and, as one of five children, she would never have received the concentrated and almost worshipping attention offered Amelia, the idolised only child in whom her mother invested so much hope and pride. Resentment and a sense of unfairness might very well have been born then, feelings which it would be impossible ever to shake off.

All this being said and every allowance made for childhood impressions, the venom of the attack on the adult Amelia eight years after her death remains to be accounted for. It may have been provoked, unwittingly, by Sarah Grand. The unexpected interview with Matilda in Tunbridge Wells took Sarah unaware and she struggled at first to remember who Matilda was. When memory returned, she hastened to prove that she was not really ignorant of her hostess's identity or her career: " 'I know you now', I confidently plunged. 'You are *My Brother's Wife*, and a great many other things' ". *My Brother's Wife* is the title of Amelia's first novel which shortly preceded *The White House by the Sea*, which was Matilda's first. Sarah could hardly have said anything more unfortunate. " 'twas ever thus!" Matilda answered after a pause. "You mistake me for my cousin Amelia Blandford Edwards. Naturally. I am moonlight to her sunshine ... I don't suppose Amelia was troubled with congratulations on being the author of my books. It was monotonously the other way. And I can't say I liked it. Or like it even now ... It does hurt", she added "with a wince". If it was the stir caused by the publication of *The Heavenly Twins* that quickened Matilda's interest in the young woman she had once met at a dinner party and which stimulated her eagerness to meet her, this meeting could not have taken place before 1893. Alternatively it might have been *The Beth Book* of 1897 which caught Matilda's attention since among other things it attacks vivisection, a cause on which Matilda felt strongly. In any case, Sarah's unlucky reference was the irritating of an old sore and the likely cause that it flared into fresh life, provoking memories all the bitterer because Matilda had by this time a long career behind her. She could have looked for the unhappy confusion of the two B's, her Betham and Amelia's Blandford, to be at last disentangled and for her years of literary labour to have ensured her recognition in her own right. The timing and bitterness of *A Suffolk Courtship* are perhaps traceable to the emotions stirred up by a well-meant but careless reference.

Prominent as the story of Inez is, it is not the only element in *A Suffolk Courtship* and soured recollection is not the only tone. The opening scene with the itinerant fiddler who has come to play for the Christmas dance evokes the old ways of a rural society which Matilda loves to trace in this book as in her other novels of the period and there is a mood of pleasant nostalgia even in the London scenes. City Road and the area about it was "no undelightful abode in those days ... Could any great thoroughfare be more animated and exhilarating than the City Road itself, any centre offer more variety and suggestion than the neighbourhood of the Angel Inn?" Among the attractions of Islington with its "glittering" High Street were the irregular houses and shrubberies of Colebrook Row where Charles Lamb lived and the flowering trees which "glorified" Percy Circus in May, while not far away was the country itself where hay-making and corn-cutting might be seen in full swing at Wood Green. In spite of the odium she attaches to no. 1 Westmoreland Square, Matilda cannot entirely suppress pleasant memories any more than she represses her sense of comedy in an account of a pioneering trial of a new-fangled shower-bath or the description of Abel Gooding's discomfort at the novel experience of a production of Shakespeare at Sadler's Wells. Revisiting the past brings a range of emotions but also the scope for lively and diverse effect. Not many, if indeed any, of her readers would recognise, except in most general terms, the background of personal reference. Frederic Harrison did not, though he caught the acrid tone. Sarah Grand did not. With all thought of Amelia and her parents put aside, *A Suffolk Courtship*, in spite of its emphasis on disenchantment, is a witty and entertaining book. *The Bookseller* reviewer of January 12th, 1901, certainly found it so, calling Susie "a charming little personage" whose love affairs "are most amusingly related". The book is "real Suffolk", he concludes, "amusing and immensely entertaining to all who are familiar with that homely county". E. A. Goodwyn in his *East Anglian Literature* of 1982 is similarly blind to the mordant ironies which permeate *A Suffolk Courtship*. Matilda was evidently subtler than Frederic Harrison realised, able to conceal the "grit" and the "heartlessness" which he deplored beneath a carapace of entertainment and offer her readers what they happily accepted as, in Harrison's words, "something ideal". *A Suffolk Courtship* is, in fact, *a roman a clef*. The key once found, it stands clear to view as a very revealing novel, suffused with the hurt and bitterness of a clever and talented woman who had never quite scaled the heights of her ambition. In the writing of it Matilda focused her frustration on one target in particular, the cousin whom she both admired and resented, for whom she felt both gratitude and affection and something like loathing. The negative feelings are worked out in the book, Matilda confident enough in her audience to know that no-one will recognise them. It may be that in the writing they are in the main exorcised, if never entirely banished. Certainly she went on to the end of her life writing and speaking in laudatory and even loving terms of the cousin who loomed so large throughout her life.

Sarah Grand, very conscious of the *faux pas* she had made at the first encounter, makes her own commentary on the relations between Matilda and Amelia whom she calls the "showier" cousin. This is an interesting adjective which may reflect hints dropped by Matilda since it could hardly have been chosen from personal experience given that, except for her notable American tour in 1889-90, Amelia lived in virtual seclusion for the last ten years of her life, applying herself unremittingly to work on behalf of the Egypt Exploration Society. Matilda had every right to be offended, Sarah writes, when new acquaintances ignored her own "admirable work" and congratulated her, instead, on

Amelia's. "The wonder was", Sarah goes on, "that it had not changed her feeling for her cousin. It had not. She delighted in Amelia's beauty, her versatility, her achievements, and spoke and wrote of her to the last with the greatest affection". No doubt Sarah believed what she wrote but she could hardly guess at the tangle of emotions which surrounded Matilda's relations with her cousin. As far as Sarah was aware the "hurt" which she had unintentionally inflicted on "the little lady" was soothed and its cause in rivalry with Amelia put aside during the late years when Matilda was pursuing a placid life in Villa Julia, cosseted by Emily Morgan, much heartened by publishers' interest in her past work and requests for more, visited by distinguished persons and applauded by those friends and neighbours whom she admitted to intimacy. Sarah Grand's comments on Matilda's appearance in age reinforce the idea of a woman at ease with life and herself, any hint of acerbity in the past now dissolved into benevolence. Comparing photographs of a younger Matilda with the woman she knew, Sarah concludes that the years have improved Matilda's looks, "made her eyes less brightly observant but more sympathetic, and softened her expression with kindliness". It is a pleasing and heartening picture to dwell on. With Amelia's death, whatever tensions there were in the relationship were ended, the portrait of Amelia-as-Inez could be supposed to have exorcised the demon of jealousy and resentment which had haunted Matilda and she could now revert without bitterness to memories of the thirty year old "close friendship" with her cousin which she writes about in *Anglo-French Reminiscences*. In response to a letter of condolence, Matilda tells Aglaia Coronio "My cousin's loss is indeed to me, very great, although of late years we did not meet often". In what seems something of a contradiction she adds: "She was here for three weeks before her fatal journey to America [1889-90] – then in full health and high spirits". Unfortunately there is no reference elsewhere to this long visit but it indicates amity at least between the cousins at that date. Whatever the outward equanimity, however, the sore place was still there and it could still be enflamed.

The chapter on Amelia which Matilda wrote for *Mid-Victorian Memories* makes full acknowledgement of her cousin's gifts and her successes as novelist and Egyptologist but it concludes with the diatribe against the "disloyalty" of women to their own sex and the repudiation of their fitness for "any public office of responsibility whatever". This outburst, a particularly strong expression of the animosity which from time to time threatens to undermine Matilda's general championship of women, comes as a rather surprising coda to the eulogy of Amelia but the sequence of ideas is clear enough. The memory of Matilda's friend, Barbara Bodichon, has not been properly honoured by her own sex, nor has that of Matilda's cousin, Amelia Edwards and, as for herself, she expected nothing more than to be overlooked too, in death as she had been in life, by the women who might have supported her. The pain of being ignored continued to "hurt" to the end and a sentence in a letter of 1909 to Clement Shorter associates it particularly with the cousin whose name casts an inescapable shadow over her own. "I feel sure", Matilda writes, "when the time comes you will not allow me to be classed as a mere appendage to my gifted relation". "A mere appendage": the choice of words is eloquent of the damage to pride and sense of achievement. The immediate cause of Matilda's rather pitiful plea to Shorter was the recent publication of a biographical dictionary in which a notice of Amelia contained the intolerably dismissive remark that "Her cousin Matilda Edwards has written several novels". She is even denied the "Betham" which she had proudly appropriated and, stubbornly defiant, never relinquished.

Coulson Kernahan, a friend of Hastings years, knew Matilda well. She could be caustic, he said, and she resented neglect "but", he adds, "of spite, meanness or malice she was incapable". It is a view of her personality fully endorsed by Sarah Grand and it is to be hoped that in the last years, after the uneven course of a lifetime devoted to work and ambitions fulfilled or disappointed, the sweet prevailed over the bitter. She had been a millionaire, she wrote, in the matter of friendships and she had friends with her at the last. She sent a final message to Sarah Grand: "Tell my friends I am quite cheerful, and tell the doctor that I never lose my good spirits. I mean to keep them to the end". It was not a bad farewell.

Amelia was less fortunate in her death. She fell down some stairs in the last stages of her American tour and she had other falls on the journey back home. Within the next few months she was operated on for suspected cancer of the left breast and though, by Kate Bradbury's account, "the dreaded evil never returned", the loss of blood, nervous exhaustion and shock weakened her beyond repair. A journey to Italy failed to restore her but the colder air of Switzerland temporarily revived her and there were hopes that the worst was over. Back in Westbury, however, she contracted influenza which turned into bronchitis and inflammation of the lung, the Edwards chest weakness revealing itself once more. Kate Bradbury was a devoted friend to the end but Mrs Braysher, the friend whose house she had shared for over thirty years, had died three months earlier in her late eighties. Amelia's illness was protracted and she died in the end on April 15th, 1892, aged sixty-one. Like Matilda, she had had several bouts of ill health in her life, some of them serious though precise causes are not always identifiable.

To some extent Matilda's life and her cousin's life run parallel. Both were self-educated and self-made women, forging their way in the world without benefit of family money or position. Both became writers of travel books and novels. Both found liberty and a more fulfilling life in other countries where they were free of the conventions and repressions imposed on women at home. Not only are their novels set largely abroad but for each of them one country held a special appeal, France for Matilda, Egypt for Amelia, and they devoted their energies and talents to its causes. Both felt keenly the injustices of English society, in relation to women and also to men of talent and promise who were denied the proper exercise of their gifts by the strictly class-bound social regime. The similarities between them are superficial only, however. Amelia wrote only eight novels, devoting two years to each and enriching them with the imaginative and intellectual depth of a powerful intelligence. When she turned to Egyptology she gave up fiction, disregarding publishers' pleas for more novels and their offers of tempting sums of money. Instead, with almost monastic dedication, she devoted herself and her talents to the pursuance of one interest above all and made an impact in her chosen field which was to be of major and lasting importance. Such single-mindedness was impossible for Matilda. The pull of the busy world was too strong, her temperament too gregarious, her impulse to involve herself with the widest possible range of people and activities too powerful for her to discipline herself to the achievement of a single goal. The sands of Egypt, as it turned out, proved a better foundation for a lasting memorial than the shifting ground of contemporary French politics.

A second important difference between the cousins is related to the first. Amelia once drew up a list of "Important People I have Known" — perhaps stung by the names which pepper Matilda's reminiscences — but she made nothing of it. In direct contrast to her cousin, she was in every respect notably reticent in everything to do with her personal life and her feelings. She could project herself into scenes of the past or the far-away with an extraordinary imaginative engagement but, as for her own life, she left only the most meagre of autobiographical accounts and these are rigidly silent about emotions or intimate personal experience. What is known or can be guessed about these has to be pieced together from her other writing or from the insights occasionally offered by others. That special quality of compelling attractiveness which naturally focused attention on her when she was young remained with her in age, as is amply demonstrated by the enthusiastic reception American audiences gave her during the 1890/91 tour. Nevertheless for the last decade of her life, the American interlude apart, she sought seclusion. Matilda on the other hand for another twenty years continued to claim attention for herself, determined never again if she could help it to be overlooked as in painful childhood memory she had been. As long as Amelia was alive she knew she would always be outshone but that years after Amelia's death she and her life's work should still be lost in her light was a bitter pill and it is no wonder that she choked over it.

In spite of all that she writes about her cousin, Matilda sheds little light on the dramatic change in Amelia's life from middle years onwards when the confident venturesome young woman changed into the semi-recluse dedicated to scholarship and service in the cause of Egyptology. Her depiction of Inez as a husband-hunting predator in *A Suffolk Courtship* has no basis in known fact or probability but it does at least seem to put out of court any suggestion that Amelia had lesbian inclinations, whether expressed or suppressed. She did have a highly emotional attachment to Marianne North, the distinguished botanical painter, but Matilda herself warns against imputing too much sexual meaning to relations between women when she explicitly rejects sexual desire as an element in the mutual attraction of Naahma and Lady Ralfe in *Mock Beggars' Hall*. The possibility remains open, nevertheless, that some psychological trauma affected Amelia's life which drove her into virtual seclusion in the last decade or so before her death and which resulted in her denying herself the physical and emotional satisfaction of a fulfilled sexual relationship. She could fascinate but she could not love is Matilda's verdict on Inez/Amelia in *A Suffolk Courtship* and perhaps she put her finger on some psychological malaise afflicting Amelia's life after the richly promising beginnings. "She does not love many people for all her seeming geniality", Kate Bradbury, close friend of Amelia in late years, remarked and there seems to be some emotional vacuum in her mature personality. Two letters written in her last illness show a pitiful, quasi-childish dependence upon an unknown younger woman. The key to all this may lie in her intense relationship with her mother in childhood and young adulthood, a relationship which Matilda highlights, and the crushing blow which her mother's death was to her. In one of her novels, *Debenham's Vow* (1870), Amelia herself analysed how an over-intense mutual devotion of mother and child could disable the child (a son in the novel) for other relationships in maturity. Certainly the maternal element is strong in Amelia's relationship with Mrs Braysher and, with the generation gap reversed, with the young woman of the last letters.

Amelia's personal life remains, in the last analysis, an enigma but the record of Matilda's relationships is more easily read. She received one proposal of marriage which, sensibly in the circumstances, she rejected and strong evidence suggests that she had an affair at some time with a Frenchman, the repercussions of which continued to reverberate at least in memory till she was old. Sarah Grand says of the Hastings years that, whereas many eminent men paid her their attentions, she never heard of any distinguished woman doing so: "but that would not strike her [Matilda] as worth mentioning", she adds, "she so very much preferred the men". One of them was Octavius Smith, a younger brother of Barbara Bodichon's father, of whom in *Mid-Victorian Memories* Matilda writes that: "In later years I owed to him the larger part of my chief pleasures in life". Octavius was the proprietor of a distillery and a very wealthy man whose lifestyle might well have been attractive to Matilda. She afterwards mysteriously adds that what began as acquaintance "afterwards grew into something more". Sarah Grand can shed no light on this since he had left the scene well before her time but "something more" is very unlikely to have meant more than close friendship. The warmth of the language is illustrative nevertheless of Matilda's partiality for her male friends.

Matilda published two volumes of poetry, in 1884 and 1907, some of them love poems written as from a male persona but love poems have traditionally been written for the expression of many feelings, ranging from political ambition to adolescent yearning, and its attractions for Matilda would be irresistible — she was a compulsive writer. She had a strong sense of rhythm, she handled rhyme dexterously and she evidently enjoyed this alternative form for expressing energy and emotion. Nothing very much of biographical significance can be deduced from her poems but one strain in them does seem to be distinctive. The situation of a deep and lasting love affair which has been denied fulfilment recurs several times and one poem, "Irrevocable", written, perhaps significantly, in a different form from the others, laments the loss of a human love which has been sacrificed for "Love Divine". The story is reminiscent of *Half-Way* and the other French novels in which Matilda bitterly inveighs against the rule of priestly celibacy and, whatever personal history may or may not have been behind it, it leaves little room for doubt that Matilda was firmly heterosexual.

Her life in its main aspects lies open for all to read. Her copious autobiographical writings seem to leave nothing unsaid and fiction and non-fiction alike are full of evidence of her doings and her personality. Her weaknesses are apparent but so also are her strengths both of character and authorship. Sarah Grand's verdict was sound. Matilda, she wrote: "If not one of the greatest ... was certainly one of the most remarkable of the group of distinguished women whom we now call Mid-Victorian". She deserves her place in any picture of this complex period, built up as it was of layer upon layer of energy, commitment and talent, much of it contributed by women. Not least of the contributors was Matilda and her name should be numbered among the brave and talented women who not only opened the way for others but registered notable achievements on their own account. As a busy and curious participant in the life of her time, a writer and an indefatigable, self-dedicated worker in the cause of international understanding and friendship, her life-story is alive with the occupations and personalities of contemporary society. Her relationship with her cousin Amelia, winding through the years but always, it would seem, coiling back to their first meeting, offers an intimate impression of psychological strains and pressures experienced by independent single women in a largely unsympathetic society. Matilda wrote them out of her system and died, we may hope, cheerful as, with characteristic firm-mindedness, she intended to do.

Works by Matilda Betham-Edwards referred to in the text

The White House by the Sea 1857
Little Bird Red and Little Bird Blue (verse drama) 1861
John and I 1862
Dr Jacob 1864
A Winter with the Swallows 1867
Through Spain to the Sahara 1868
Kitty 1869
The Sylvestres 1871
Felicia 1875
Bridget 1877
Brother Gabriel 1878
Six Life Stories of Famous Women 1880
Forestalled 1880
Pearla 1883
Half-Way 1886
Next of Kin Wanted 1887
The Parting of the Ways 1888
For One and the World 1889
A Romance of the Wire 1891
Edition of Arthur Young's *Travels in France* 1892
Romance of a French Parsonage 1892
France of To-Day 1892
The Curb of Honour 1893
A Romance of Dijon 1894
The Golden Bee and other Recitations 1895
Autobiography of Arthur Young 1898
The Lord of the Harvest 1899
Anglo-French Reminiscences 1900
A Suffolk Courtship 1900
Mock Beggars' Hall 1902
Barham Brocklebank 1903
A Humble Lover 1903
Home Life in France 1905
Martha Rose 1906
Poems 1907
A Close Ring 1907
Literary Rambles in France 1907
Friendly Faces of Three Nationalities 1911
In French Africa 1912
From an Islington Window 1914
Hearts of Alsace 1916
Twentieth Century France 1917
French Fireside Poetry 1919
Mid-Victorian Memories 1919

Select Bibliography

Black Helen C., *Notable Women Authors of the Day*, London 1906. Chapter on Matilda Betham-Edwards originally published in *The Lady's Pictorial*, 1891.

Brodribb, Gerald, *Hastings and Men of Letters*, Old Hastings Preservation Society, 1971.

Glyde, John, *Suffolk in the Nineteenth Century*, London, 1855.

Goodwyn, E. A., *East Anglian Literature, A Survey from Crabbe to Adrian Bell*, privately printed 1982.

Harrison, Frederic, obituary in *The Positivist Review*, vol 27, 1919.

Kaye-Smith, Sheila *All the Books of my Life*, Cassell, 1956.

Kernahan, Coulson, *Celebrities*, London, 1923.

Parkin, Thomas, Obituary in *The Hastings and St Leonards Observer*, 11.1.1919.

Robinson, Jane, *Wayward Women*, O.U.P 1990.

Thirsk, J. and Imray, J., *Suffolk Farming in the Nineteenth Century*, Ipswich, 1958.

Tolhurst, Peter, *East Anglia: a Literary Pilgrimage*, Black Dog Books, 1996.

Wojtczak, Helena, *Notable Women of Victorian Hastings*, The Hastings Press, 2002.